Palette of Color Monograph Series

The Chemistry of Food Dyes

by Dianne N. Epp

Series Editor
Mickey Sarquis, Director
Center for Chemistry Education

Terrific Science Press™
Miami University Middletown
Middletown, Ohio

This monograph is intended for use by teachers, chemists, and properly supervised students. Teachers and other users must develop and follow procedures for the safe handling, use, and disposal of chemicals in accordance with local and state regulations and requirements. The cautions, warnings, and safety reminders associated with the doing of experiments and activities involving the use of chemicals and equipment contained in this publication have been compiled from sources believed to be reliable and to represent the best opinion on the subject as of 1995. However, no warranty, guarantee, or representation is made by the author, the editor, or the Terrific Science Press as to the correctness or sufficiency of any information herein. Neither the author, editor, nor publisher assumes any responsibility or liability for the use of the information herein, nor can it be assumed that all necessary warnings and precautionary measures are contained within this publication. Other or additional information or measures may be required or desirable because of particular or exceptional conditions or circumstances, or because of new or changed legislation.

Terrific Science Press
Miami University Middletown
4200 East University Blvd.
Middletown, Ohio 45042
513/727-3269
www.terrificscience.org

ISBN: 1-883822-07-6

The publisher takes no responsibility for the use of any materials or methods described in this book, nor for the products thereof. Permission is granted to copy materials for classroom use.

This material is based upon work supported by the National Science Foundation. Any opinions, findings, and conclusions or recommendations expressed in this material are those of the author and do not necessarily reflect the views of the National Science Foundation.

Contents

Acknowledgments

The author and editor wish to thank the following individuals who have contributed to the development of *The Chemistry of Food Dyes.*

Technical Consultant

Carol Riddle   Hilton Davis Company   Cincinnati, OH

Terrific Science Press Design and Production Team

Susan Gertz, Amy Stander, Stephen Gentle, Thomas Nackid, Lisa Taylor, Anne Munson, Andrea Nolan

Reviewers

Susan Hershberger   Miami University   Oxford, OH
Harold J. McKone   Saint Joseph College   West Hartford, CT
Linda Woodward   University of Southwestern Louisiana   Lafayette, LA

Dedication

To Alain, Sonia and Samuel and
To Rachel and Tim
Who have all added immeasurably to my life.

Foreword

The Chemistry of Food Dyes is the third in a three-volume series of monographs entitled *Palette of Color.* This series is aimed at enabling high school chemistry teachers to introduce their students to a fascinating area of industrial chemistry—dyes and colorants. These monographs provide background information on the history and chemistry of various dyes and colorants, together with hands-on activities on producing, testing, and using these chemicals. Dianne Epp has brought together an excellent collection of chemistry activities in a format that is convenient and easy to use. As in all volumes published by Terrific Science Press, each of these activities has been tested by teachers in the Center for Chemistry Education's (CCE) Terrific Science Programs and reviewed by experts in the field to ensure accuracy, safety, and pedagogical effectiveness. We believe that these monographs will enhance the relevance and appeal of the high school chemistry teacher's repertoire.

Dianne created these volumes while on a 1993–94 sabbatical from East High School in Lincoln, NE. During that year, Dianne joined the CCE team as a Teacher Fellow and worked on this and other curriculum-development efforts, including integrating microscale laboratory activities into Miami University's general chemistry curriculum. We thank Dianne for sharing her keen insights into the topics of dye chemistry, microscale chemistry, and chemical education; for her hard work in developing this series; and for allowing us to publish it. Thanks also to Hilton Davis Company and to Carol Riddle of Hilton Davis for the contribution of her time as a technical consultant during the development of *The Chemistry of Food Dyes.*

In addition to the *Palette of Color* monograph series, the CCE offers many other science education opportunities and resource materials for teachers and students at all levels. While each initiative within the Center has a unique focus and addresses the needs of a distinct population, all programs emphasize hands-on, inquiry-based chemical education through which students develop their abilities to work together to solve scientific challenges, think critically, and utilize their powers of observation. Learn more about the Center at *www.terrificscience.org.*

We hope you will find that these monographs provide you with a useful and exciting way to involve your students in doing chemistry through integrated real-world themes. We welcome your comments at any time and are interested in learning about especially successful uses of these materials.

Mickey Sarquis, Director
Center for Chemistry Education
June 1995

What Are the *Palette of Color* Monographs?

Look around you—color is everywhere. The clothes we wear, the food we eat, the posters with which we decorate our rooms; indeed all of our surroundings, natural and man-made, abound with color. From prehistoric times people have been fascinated with color; from cave paintings to the latest computers, color has been our constant companion.

The *Palette of Color* monograph series enables high school chemistry teachers to challenge students to explore the chemistry behind dyes. Each monograph examines a different class of dyes and investigates the chemistry using principles common to most high school chemistry curricula. Hands-on, problem-solving activities involve students in answering questions posed about the dyes and their uses.

The Chemistry of Vat Dyes

Indigo and Inkodyes are used to illustrate how vat dyes are synthesized and used. Until the end of the 19th century, all colors were obtained from natural sources, but today the number of synthetic colorants exceeds 7,000. One class of these colorants, the vat dyes, contains not only the oldest natural dyes known, but also many important synthetic dyes. This class of dyes is studied in this monograph.

The Chemistry of Natural Dyes

For thousands of years, dyes were obtained from natural sources, such as plants and animals. In spite of the fact that synthetic dyes have replaced many natural dyes for commercial use, natural dyes still hold a fascination and are used extensively by artisans around the world. This monograph investigates the most common type of natural dyes, known as acid or anionic dyes, and their reactions with wool and eggshells.

The Chemistry of Food Dyes

Dyes aren't just for fabrics—colorants have been added to food for centuries to enhance its appearance. This monograph investigates both the compounds which give foods their natural color and the synthetic colorants currently approved for use in foods.

How to Use *The Chemistry of Food Dyes*

The *Palette of Color* monographs are intended for use by a secondary chemistry teacher. A monograph may be inserted into the curriculum when the appropriate chemistry concept is being examined as a practical application of that concept. Monographs might also be used as independent study units for students.

Each monograph is organized in two parts: Teacher Background Information and Classroom Materials. The Teacher Background Information section includes a review of pertinent science content, notes and setups for the activities, and cross-curricular activities to supplement the science activities. The Classroom Materials section includes student background and activity handouts and overheads.

What's in *The Chemistry of Food Dyes*

Dyes aren't just for fabrics—colorants have been added to food for centuries to enhance its appearance. This monograph investigates both the compounds which give foods their natural color and the synthetic colorants currently approved for use in foods.

What Students Do

In this monograph, students do the following:

- study the chemistry of natural food colorants and examine experimentally the chemical stability of these colorants;
- study the chemistry of synthetic food colorants and examine experimentally the chemical stability of these colorants;
- use chromatography to identify the colorants present in consumer products such as nontoxic markers, Kool-Aid® and Easter-egg dyes; and
- carry out the synthesis of a synthetic food colorant, FD&C Yellow No. 6, and confirm its identity by chromatography.

Key Ideas

The following key ideas are covered:

- chemical structures and stability of various food colorants;
- chromatography as an identification tool; and
- synthesis and identification of an organic compound.

Time Frame

Teachers should select from the variety of activities to fit the time available. A minimum of three 50-minute lessons would be needed to cover the topic of food dyes.

Employing Appropriate Safety Procedures

Experiments, demonstrations, and hands-on activities add relevance, fun, and excitement to science education at any level. However, even the simplest activity can become dangerous when the proper safety precautions are ignored or when the activity is done incorrectly or performed by students without proper supervision. While the activities in this book include cautions, warnings, and safety reminders from sources believed to be reliable and while the text has been extensively reviewed by classroom teachers and university scientists, it is your responsibility to develop and follow procedures for the safe execution of the activities you choose to do. You are also responsible for the safe handling, use, and disposal of chemicals in accordance with local and state regulations and requirements.

Safety First

- Collect and read the Materials Safety Data Sheets (MSDS) for all of the chemicals used in your experiments. MSDS's provide physical property data, toxicity information, and handling and disposal specifications for chemicals. They can be obtained upon request from manufacturers and distributors of these chemicals. In fact, MSDS's are often shipped with chemicals when they are ordered. These should be collected and made available to students, faculty, or parents for information about specific chemicals used in these activities.

- Read and follow the American Chemical Society Minimum Safety Guidelines for Chemical Demonstrations on the next page. Remember that you are a role model for your students—your attention to safety will help them develop good safety habits while assuring that everyone has fun with these activities.

- Read each activity carefully and observe all safety precautions and disposal procedures. Determine and follow all local and state regulations and requirements.

- Never attempt an activity if you are unfamiliar or uncomfortable with the procedures or materials involved. Consult a college or industrial chemist for advice or ask him or her to perform the activity for your class. These people are often delighted to help.

- Always practice activities yourself before using them with your class. This is the only way to become thoroughly familiar with an activity, and familiarity will help prevent potentially hazardous (or merely embarrassing) mishaps. In addition, you may find variations that will make the activity more meaningful to your students.

- You, your assistants, and any students participating in the preparation for or doing of the activity must wear safety goggles if indicated in the activity and at any other time you deem necessary.

- Special safety instructions are not given for everyday classroom materials being used in a typical manner. Use common sense when working with hot, sharp, or breakable objects. Keep tables or desks covered to avoid stains. Keep spills cleaned up to avoid falls.

ACS Minimum Safety Guidelines for Chemical Demonstrations

This section outlines safety procedures that Chemical Demonstrators must follow at all times.

1. Know the properties of the chemicals and the chemical reactions involved in all demonstrations presented.

2. Comply with all local rules and regulations.

3. Wear appropriate eye protection for all chemical demonstrations.

4. Warn the members of the audience to cover their ears whenever a loud noise is anticipated.

5. Plan the demonstration so that harmful quantities of noxious gases (e.g., NO_2, SO_2, H_2S) do not enter the local air supply.

6. Provide safety shield protection wherever there is the slightest possibility that a container, its fragments, or its contents could be propelled with sufficient force to cause personal injury.

7. Arrange to have a fire extinguisher at hand whenever the slightest possibility for fire exists.

8. Do not taste or encourage spectators to taste any non-food substance.

9. Never use demonstrations in which parts of the human body are placed in danger (such as placing dry ice in the mouth or dipping hands into liquid nitrogen).

10. Do not use "open" containers of volatile, toxic substances (e.g., benzene, CCl_4, CS_2, formaldehyde) without adequate ventilation as provided by fume hoods.

11. Provide written procedure, hazard, and disposal information for each demonstration whenever the audience is encouraged to repeat the demonstration.

12. Arrange for appropriate waste containers for and subsequent disposal of materials harmful to the environment.

Part A: Teacher Background Information

What Are Food Dyes?

Notes and Setups for Activities

Supplementary Activities

References

What Are Food Dyes?

Natural Colorants

Colors extracted from naturally occurring materials have been added to food for centuries to enhance its appearance. Food colorants are used to improve the appearance of foods which have lost color due to processing or to give color to naturally colorless foods. Colorants that are extracted from natural materials or that are identical chemically to natural colorants are exempt from government certification. Three natural colorants are discussed here: carotenoids, chlorophylls, and anthocyanins.

Carotenoids

The carotenoids are one of the most important groups of natural materials used as food colorants. This group includes carotenes, which are strictly hydrocarbons, and xanthophylls, which are similar in structure to carotenes but also contain oxygen. Carotenoids contribute to the vivid red, yellow, and orange colors of many fruits, seeds, and roots.

One example of a carotenoid that has been used as a food colorant in the United States and Europe for over 100 years is the orange-yellow, oil-soluble coloring material found in annatto. Annatto is extracted from the seed of the *Bixa orellana L.* tree found mainly in Central and South America. Compared to other carotenoids, annatto is surprisingly stable to air oxidation. Its stability to heat and pH changes also enhances its usefulness.

The major colorant in annatto is bixin. The structure of its stable trans form (also called isobixin) is shown in Figure A1. Bixin is a brownish-red crystalline material, but when used at various concentrations in foods such as butter and cheese, it ranges in yellow hues from butter yellow to peach. The color of the various carotenoids results from the extensive series of alternating double bonds in the molecules. The greater the number of double bonds, the more red the pigment will appear. A yellow color is present if the compound contains at least seven double bonds; with more than seven double bonds the color will go toward orange and then red.

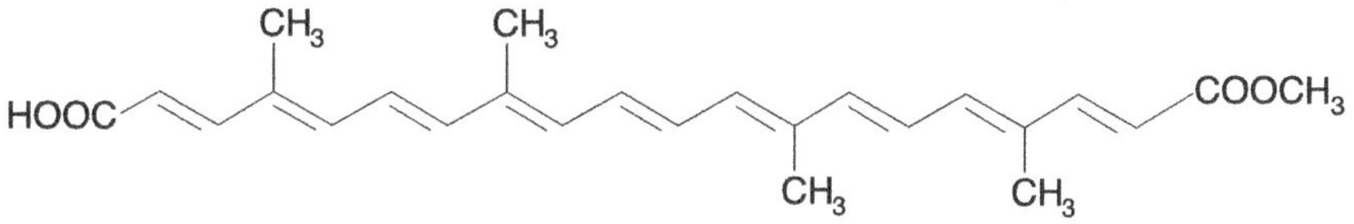

Figure A1: Bixin, the yellow colorant of annatto

Beta-carotene (β-carotene) is one of the few carotenoids which has been prepared synthetically for use as a food colorant. Because of its intense orange color it may be used effectively at very low concentrations (1–10 parts per million). It is used to color foods such as margarine, salad dressings, ice cream, cheese, pasta, and bakery goods.

β-carotene is an important precursor of vitamin A. Through a sequence of reactions (See Figure A2), β-carotene is connected to retinin, which can in turn be converted to vitamin A.

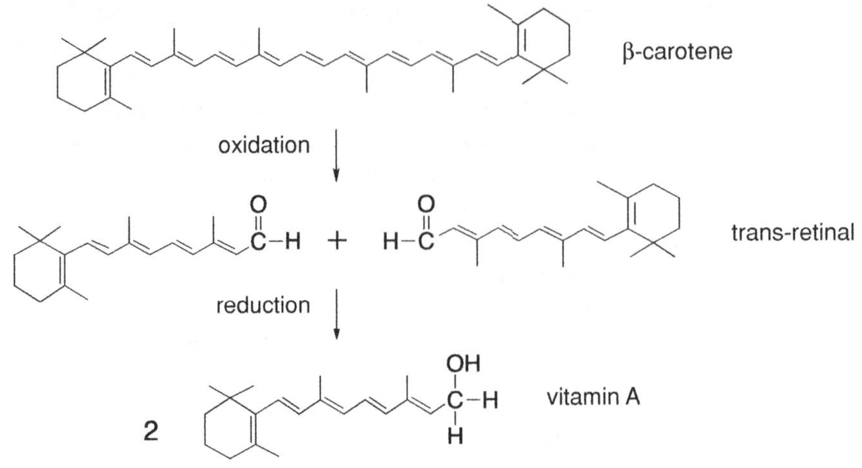

Figure A2: Formation of vitamin A from β-carotene

Lycopene is another simple carotene. (See Figure A3.) This is the bright red colorant present in tomato extracts.

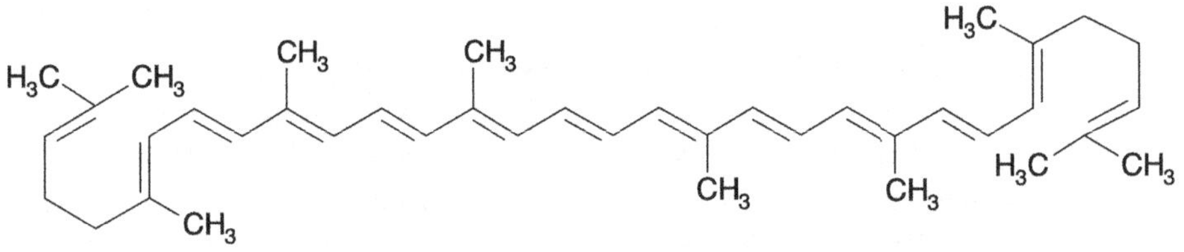

Figure A3: Lycopene, the red colorant in tomatoes

Chlorophylls

Chlorophylls, the most abundant plant pigment, are responsible for the green pigments in most vegetables, leaves, and fruits. In addition to providing color, chlorophylls are an important catalyst in photosynthesis. There are two principal types of chlorophylls: chlorophyll a, which is bluish-green, and chlorophyll b, which is more yellow-green. (See Figure A4.)

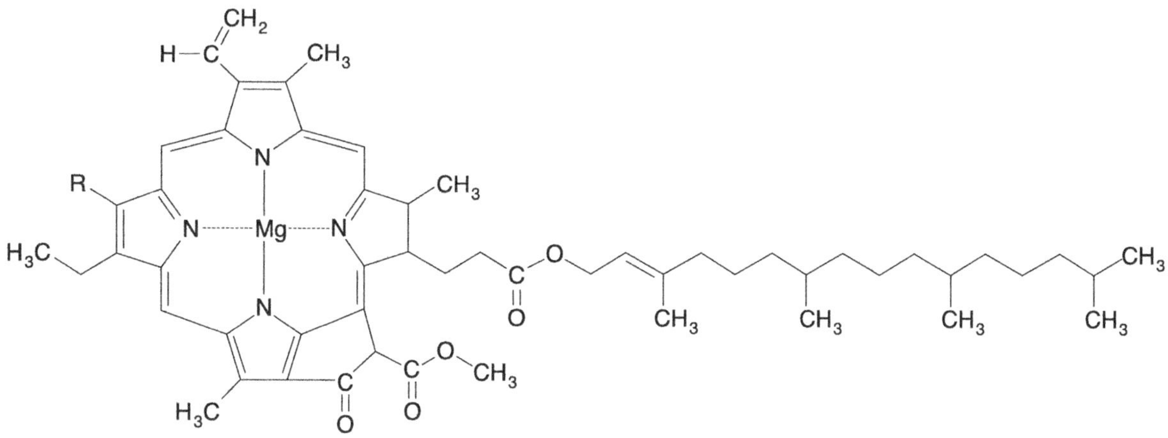

Figure A4: Chlorophylls a and b, responsible for the green color in many vegetables
(chlorophyll a: R = CH₃; chlorophyll b: R = CHO)

When green vegetables are heated in even mildly acidic conditions, the magnesium ion is replaced by protons. This reaction yields a class of compounds known as the pheophytins, which have a dirty brown color and are responsible for the dull "overcooked" color of green vegetables that have been subjected to extended heating. Since the plant cell content is slightly acidic, pheophytin formation is hard to avoid, especially during the canning process. A derivative of chlorophyll in which the central magnesium ion is replaced by copper and the ester side chain removed to form the sodium salt is now being used as a food colorant. This compound is fairly water soluble, has an acceptable blue-green color, and, most important, survives prolonged heating during the canning process.

Anthocyanins

Anthocyanins are responsible for the pink, red, violet, and blue colors of fruits and vegetables. Anthocyanins are organic compounds that are usually found in the sap of epidermal plant cells. This group of compounds has very complex structures that vary widely. However, most anthocyanins found in nature contain the basic three-ring structure shown in Figure A5. This three-ring molecule structure is called a flavylium ion.

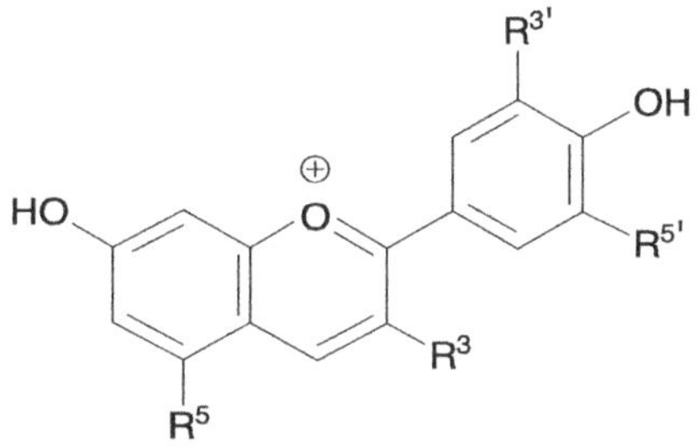

Figure A5: Flavylium ion, the principal structural unit in anthocyanins.

R indicates the typical site of the sugar residue.

Anthocyanins typically contain one or more sugar molecules attached at either the R^3 or R^5 position (or both). In addition, sometimes acyl groups are attached to the sugar molecules. (See Figure A6.)

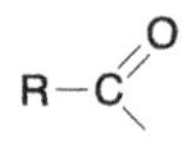

Figure A6: The structure of an acyl group

Hydroxyl (–OH) and methoxy (–OCH$_3$) groups can also substitute at the R locations not otherwise containing the sugar residue. The number of these hydroxyl and methoxy groups influences the color of the anthocyanins. More hydroxyl groups cause the color to become more blue; more methoxy groups increase redness. Figure A7 shows the structure of one of the eight anthocyanins present in red cabbage.

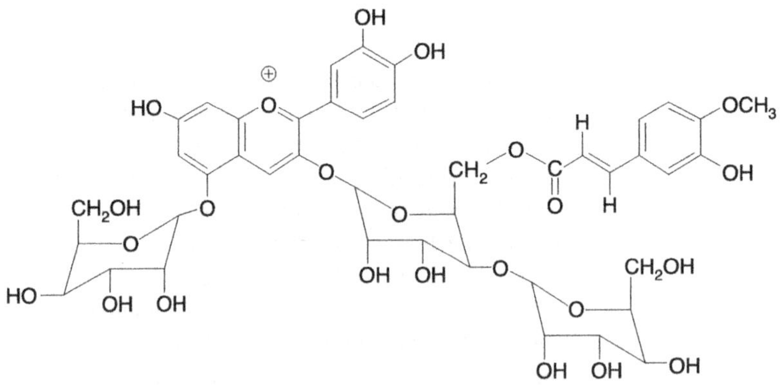

Figure A7: One of the anthocyanins present in red cabbage

The complex behavior of anthocyanins with regard to pH, shown in Figure A8, has been a subject of much investigation. When the anthocyanin is extracted into an aqueous solution of low pH (1–3), the color is always red. This is due to the protonated form, called the flavylium salt. At a high pH (greater than 10) the color is yellow due to the breakdown of the three-ring structure to form a chalcone derivative. However, interesting changes occur at pH levels between these extremes. If the pH of the red flavylium salt (pH 1–3) is changed to approximately pH 8, a dramatic, rapid color change to blue or bluish-purple occurs. This change is extremely fast and results from the acid-base neutralization of the flavylium ion to one of two possible anhydro base forms. However, if the pH of flavylium salt (pH 1–3) is changed to 4–5, a much slower but thermodynamically favored product, colorless carbinol, is formed.

*Figure A8: Anthocyanin changes with pH variations
(adapted from S. Thompson)*

Anthocyanins are playing an increasingly larger role as a colorant material for various foods. Anthocyanins are fairly heat stable and resist fading in daylight. In the latter case, anthocyanins are superior to synthetic reds which tend to fade substantially in light. Black grapes provide the major source of anthocyanins by weight for use as food colorants. Pure grape pigments have been tested and are successfully being used to color canned fruit, fruit syrups, yogurt, and other products. Cranberry pulp and skins have also been used as natural colorants since 40% of the original fruit anthocyanin is still present, even after double pressing to extract the juice.

Synthetic Colorants

Synthetic colorants rapidly replaced natural food colorants following the discovery of mauvine by William Perkin in 1856. In many cases, synthetic colorants proved superior to their natural counterparts, providing a more intense color, consistency of shade, stability, and ease of application. Unfortunately, because the toxic nature of these synthetic colorants was poorly understood initially, their widespread use led to unforeseen problems. (For examples of problems that occurred and additional details on the history of this activity, see Student Background 1.)

As toxicological and testing methods improved, a series of laws were enacted to regulate the use of synthetic food colorants. The general regulatory categories for synthetic colorants are: FD&C colors, which are certified for use in coloring foods, drugs, and cosmetics; D&C colors, which are considered safe in drugs and cosmetics when ingested or in contact with mucous membranes; and Ext. D&C colors, which are for external use only. This monograph centers on the FD&C colors which are certified for use in foods.

Though regulations vary, most countries not only have an approved list of permitted food colors but also have purity specifications that stipulate minimum color and maximum impurity levels for trace metals, such as arsenic and lead; water-insoluble impurities; and breakdown products. In the United States, every batch of color is tested by the FDA against their specifications. The color manufacturer sends a sample of each batch to the FDA laboratories in Washington, DC, and upon completion of satisfactory analysis, the batch is assigned a certified lot number.

There are only seven certified FD&C colorants. These structures are shown in Figure A9. The water solubility of these molecules is due to the presence of a number of sodium carboxylate and sodium sulfonate groups on each. The anions of these salts are highly colored which accounts for their classification as anionic dyes.

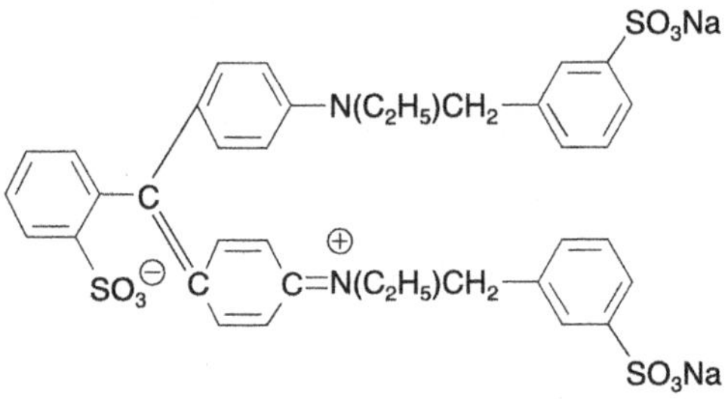

FD&C Blue No.1

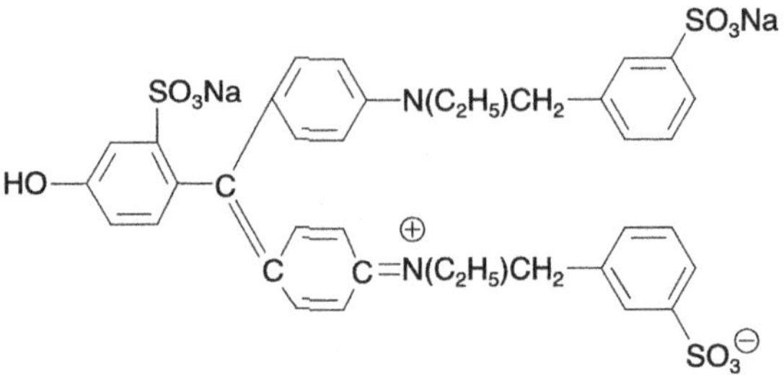

FD&C Green No. 3

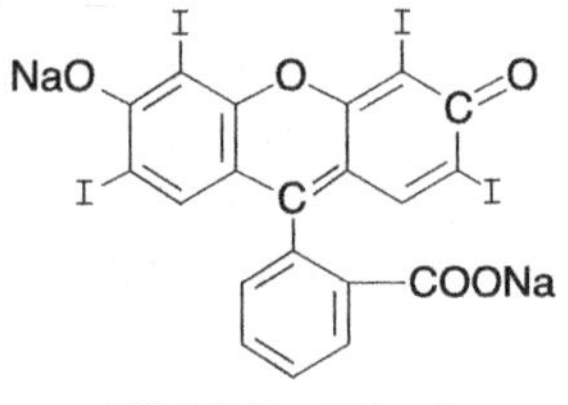

FD&C Red No. 3

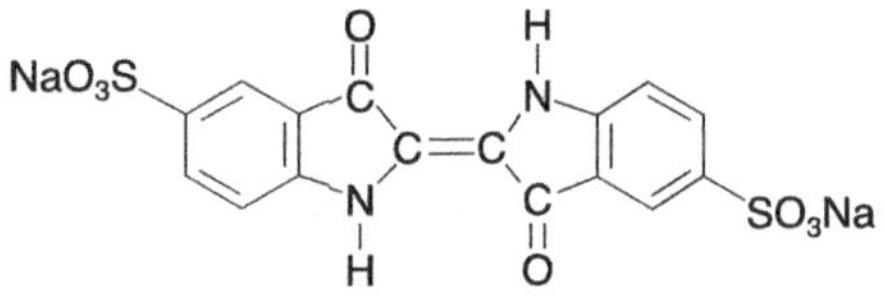

FD&C Blue No. 2

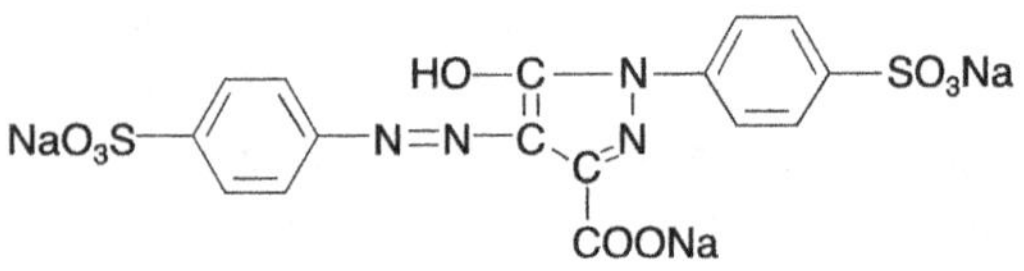

FD&C Yellow No. 5

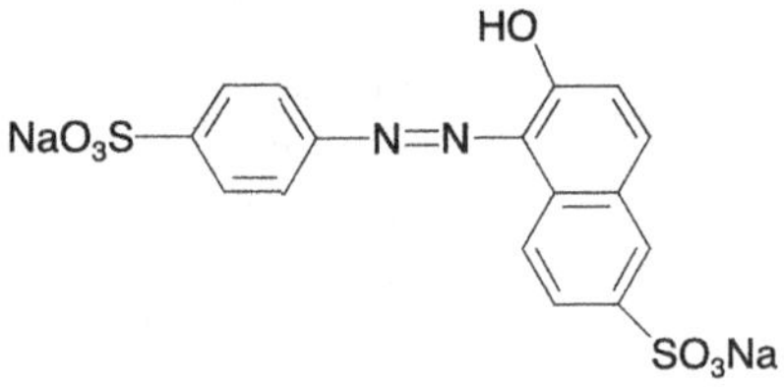

FD&C Yellow No. 6

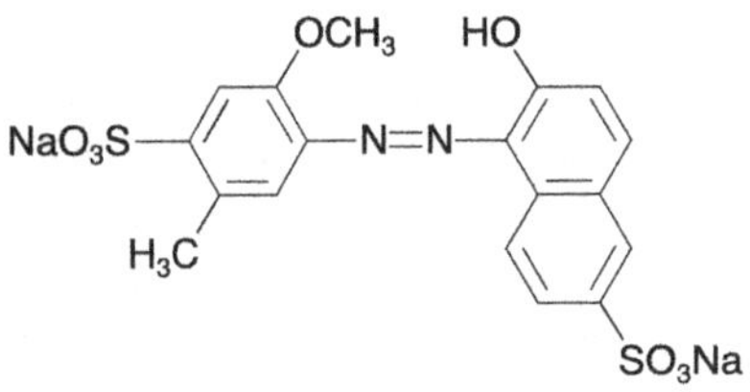

FD&C Red No. 40

Figure A9: FD&C colorants

FD&C colors are classified according to their chromophoric (color-giving) groups—azo, triarylmethane, pyrazolone, indigo, and xanthene. See Figure A10 for the structures of these groups.

Figure A10: Chromophores of FD&C colorants

One of the primary requirements for a food colorant is stability under various conditions. Stability to acids and bases varies considerably. Azo dyes are the most stable to pH changes. Additionally, not all colorants can be used at all pH ranges; FD&C Red No. 3, for example, precipitates from acidic solutions, and FD&C Green No. 3 turns blue under basic conditions.

Strong sunlight has a destructive effect on some colorants so, as much as possible, colored foodstuffs are protected from direct exposure to light. All commonly used food colorants are affected by oxidizing and reducing agents. Ascorbic acid, for example, is a relatively strong reducing agent which is frequently added to foods as an antioxidant and as a vitamin C source. Because of its reducing capabilities, careful studies of color stability must be made for foods in which it is present. In canned goods, any acidic component in the food may attack the metal container and produce reducing conditions which may destroy color. Some sugars also have a reducing effect on food colors.

Food colors may be unstable at the high temperatures used in food processing and preservation. All synthetic colors are added as late in the manufacturing process as possible, after most of the heating has taken place.

Because water-soluble FD&C colors are very useful in water-based foodstuffs such as beverages or gelatin desserts, but have limited use in fatty foods, water-insoluble "lakes" are used to color fat- or oil-based foods such as ice cream, cake fillings, icing, and coated candies. Lakes are made by precipitating the aluminum or calcium salt of a certified food colorant onto a substratum of alumina. (See Figure A11.) Lakes are used as dispersions in various carriers such as edible oils and glycerine which can then be mixed with the product to be colored.

$$3(\text{Dye—SO}_3\text{Na}) \; + \; \text{AlCl}_3 \longrightarrow (\text{Dye—SO}_3^{\ominus})_3 \, \text{Al}^{\oplus 3+} \; + \; 3\text{NaCl}$$

FD&C colorant

deposited onto
$\text{Al}_2\text{O}_3 \cdot 3\text{H}_2\text{O}$
to form lake

Figure A11: Manufacture of colored lakes

Though only seven primary colorants are currently certified for use in foods, a wide range of secondary or blended shades may be prepared by creating mixtures of the primary food color powders. Food colors are available in the traditional dry powder form, which is water soluble. Extremely fine powder is used to color dry drink powders and instant dessert mixes. For some uses, especially to color solutions, granules of the colorant may be used. These are more easily handled in the manufacturing process.

The cost of manufacturing synthetic colorants depends on the cost of raw materials, production costs, and supply and demand. In addition, one must add the cost of ensuring ultrahigh purity and the cost of certification. Thus colorants that are to be used in foods are much more expensive than typical dyes destined for textile use. Fortunately, very little colorant is generally required to achieve the desired results, so the cost of the colorant adds little to the overall consumer cost of a product.

■ Notes and Setups for Activities

Activity 1: How Does Color Affect Our Perception of Food?

Students examine the role color plays in identifying and choosing foods.

Safety and Disposal

These experiments involve the preparation of food products and must NOT be carried out in the chemistry lab. Acceptable alternatives are the school's food lab, cafeteria, or a standard classroom that has been properly cleaned. Laboratory equipment must not be used to prepare food samples. Measuring cups, bowls, and pans should be borrowed from the home economics department of the school or brought from home. Sanitation should be carefully maintained.

Part 1: How Do Color Clues Help Identify Flavors?

The entire class may act as the "test panel" with the teacher preparing small samples of the beverages in disposable paper cups. Alternatively, the class may be divided into two groups, one to prepare samples and the other group to be the test panel. In this case, roles should be exchanged for the second part of Activity 1 so that all students will have a chance to be part of a test panel. Beverages should be cold, if possible, as this will make differences in flavor more challenging to recognize. Devise a code for each flavor and mark the cups with the appropriate codes.

Materials

- disposable paper cups
- several colorless commercial carbonated beverages such as New York Seltzers, Clearly Canadian, and colorless colas

Part 2: Do "Wrong" Color Clues Tend to Confuse Flavors?

Since time is required for the gelatin to harden, you may want to prepare or have the students prepare the samples a day before the test will be carried out.

Materials

Enough to make two square 8-inch pans. If more is needed, double the amounts.

- 2 packets unflavored gelatin
- ⅓ cup sugar
- saucepan for heating water
- 2 square 8-inch cake pans
- spoon
- measuring cup
- food colors

- flavoring extracts
- hot plate
- knife for cutting gelatin blocks

Part 3: Is Color a Factor in the Choice of Foods?

The teacher can prepare sherbet samples and treat a panel of students as "consumers" in a taste test. Alternatively, the class may choose to gather a larger pool of data by setting up a table in the lunch room and performing a school-wide survey. Discuss with the class how a company would need to set up such a test so that the results would be valid and not "prejudiced."

Materials

- frozen sherbet made as described in Getting Ready
- disposable cups and spoons for serving frozen sherbet

Getting Ready

Prepare two recipes of frozen sherbet using the following recipe.

Recipe for Sherbet*

Mix: 1 can evaporated milk, thoroughly chilled

        ⅔ cup sugar

Add: 3 tablespoons lemon juice or lime juice

        Beat until stiff. Freeze until firm.

* The recipe can be increased as needed.

If you are using lemon juice, add yellow food color to one recipe. If you are using lime juice, add green food color.

Source: Longacre, D.J. *More-With-Less Cookbook;* Herald: Scottdale, PA, 1981.

Activity 2: How Stable Are Natural Colors?

This experiment investigates the stability of natural colors that occur in foods. Various conditions are tested: pH buffers of pH 2 and 12 are used to investigate acidic and basic conditions, calcium chloride ($CaCl_2$) simulates reaction with "hard" water, oxidizing conditions are provided by a solution of Clorox® and water, and the effect of a reducing agent is shown by reaction with sodium thiosulfate ($Na_2S_2O_3$). The natural colorants suggested are beet extract, a betalin; turmeric, a dione; and the anthocyanins from grape and cranberry.

Safety and Disposal

Eye protection must be worn for this experiment and during the preparation of the test solutions. Avoid skin or eye contact with all solutions used in the activity and the reagents used to make these solutions. If contact occurs, wash the affected area thoroughly with running water. If the contact involves the eyes, flush the eyes continually with running water for 15 minutes and seek medical assistance while rinsing is occurring. When preparing basic or acidic solutions, always add the base or the acid to water.

Materials

Per pair of students
- 24-well plastic microscale reaction plate
- 6 plastic transfer pipets filled with test liquids
- distilled water (Deionized water can be substituted.)
- 11.1 g calcium chloride ($CaCl_2$)
- 10 mL commercial Clorox
- 15.8 g sodium thiosulfate ($Na_2S_2O_3$)
- pH 2 solution purchased or made from 17 drops of 12M hydrochloric acid (HCl) and distilled water
- pH 12 solution purchased or made from 0.4 g solid sodium hydroxide, NaOH (approximately 4 pellets), and distilled water

Solutions of a known pH may be purchased from Flinn Scientific, P.O. Box 219, Batavia, IL 60510-0219 or made as described in Getting Ready.

- 4 empty plastic transfer pipets
- 4 50-mL beakers
- glass stirring rod
- metal spatula
- small funnel and filter paper
- small piece of beet
- 1 spoonful turmeric
- 1 spoonful grape juice concentrate
- 3–4 cranberries (frozen or fresh)
- sheet of white paper
- toothpick
- 15 mL 50/50 isopropyl alcohol (commercial rubbing alcohol/water by volume)
- goggles for each student

Getting Ready

Prepare test solutions as follows:

1. Prepare a 1 M $CaCl_2$ solution by dissolving 11.1 g $CaCl_2$ in distilled water to a final volume of 100 mL.

2. Prepare a 10% Clorox solution by dissolving 10 mL commercial Clorox in distilled water to a final volume of 100 mL.

3. Prepare a 1 M $Na_2S_2O_3$ solution by dissolving 15.8 g $Na_2S_2O_3$ in distilled water to a final volume of 100 mL.

4. If not purchased, prepare a pH 2 solution by dissolving 17 drops of 12 M HCl in 800 mL distilled water and diluting to 1 L.

5. If not purchased, prepare a pH 12 solution by dissolving 0.4 g NaOH (approximately 4 pellets) in 800 mL distilled water and dilute to 1 L.

6. For each pair of students, fill six transfer pipets with the six test liquids (the solutions prepared in Steps 1–5 and the distilled water) and label appropriately.

Results

The following are given as one set of typical data.

Typical Results for Activity 2						
natural sample	distilled water	pH 2 solution	pH 12 solution	1 M $CaCl_2$ (aq)	10% Clorox	1 M $Na_2S_2O_3$ (aq)
beet	red	NC*	yellow	NC*	colorless	NC*
turmeric	yellow	NC*	red-orange	NC*	colorless	NC*
grape	purple	deep red	green	NC*	colorless	precipitate
cranberry	red	deep red	light green	NC*	colorless	precipitate
*NC=no change						

Answers to Summary Questions

1. Natural colors decolorize rapidly under oxidizing conditions. The colors from grape juice and cranberry (anthocyanins) also decolorize under reducing conditions.

2. The major color changes occur under basic conditions.

3. Turmeric and beet appear to give colors that are fairly stable, but even these bleach immediately under oxidizing conditions.

4. If basic conditions are used, these will change color. Also, both beet and turmeric have a pronounced flavor (the students might note the odor) which could affect the foodstuff.

5. The sodium bicarbonate is a basic substance which reacts locally with the cranberries to cause a color change from red to green.

Activity 3: How Stable Are Synthetic Food Colors?

This experiment investigates the stability of synthetic food colors in hard water and under acidic, basic, oxidizing, and reducing conditions. The FD&C Colors suggested for this experiment are Red No. 3, Yellow No. 6, Blue No. 1, and Red No. 40. FD&C certified colors may be obtained from Noveon Hilton-Davis, Inc., Cincinnati, OH 45237; 513/841-4000; *http://www.noveoninc.com.*

Safety and Disposal

Eye protection must be worn for this experiment and during the preparation of the test solutions. Avoid skin or eye contact of all solutions used in the activity and the reagents used to make these solutions. If contact occurs, wash the affected area thoroughly with running water. If the contact involves the eyes, flush the eyes continually with running water for 15 minutes and seek medical assistance while rinsing is occurring. When preparing basic or acidic solutions, always add the base or the acid to water.

Materials

Per pair of students
- 24-well plastic microscale reaction plate
- 10 plastic transfer pipets
- distilled water (Deionized water can be substituted.)
- 11.1 g calcium chloride ($CaCl_2$)
- 10 mL commercial Clorox
- 15.8 g sodium thiosulfate ($Na_2S_2O_3$)
- pH 2 solution purchased or made from 17 drops of 12M hydrochloric acid (HCl) and distilled water
- pH 12 solution purchased or made from 0.4 g solid sodium hydroxide, NaOH (approximately 4 pellets), and distilled water
- FD&C Yellow No. 6
- FD&C Red No. 3
- FD&C Blue No. 1
- FD&C Red No. 40
- white sheet of paper
- toothpick
- goggles for each student

Getting Ready

Prepare the test solutions as described in Activity 2, Getting Ready. Stock solutions of the FD&C colorants should be approximately 1% by weight or fairly deeply colored, but not so dark that they are no longer transparent.

Results

The following are given as one set of typical data.

FD&C sample	distilled water	pH 2 solution	pH 12 solution	1 M CaCl$_2$ (aq)	10% Clorox	1 M Na$_2$S$_2$O$_3$ (aq)
Typical Results for Activity 3						
Yellow No. 6	yellow-orange	orange	dark orange-brown	slight ppt.	colorless	slightly darker
Red No. 3	pinkish-red	ppt.	red	ppt.	colorless	slightly redder
Blue No. 1	blue	NC*	NC*	NC*	colorless	NC*
Red No. 40	red	NC*	orange	NC*	colorless	orange
*NC=no change						

Answers to Summary Questions

1. Blue No. 1 appears to be the most stable; it was unaffected except in the Clorox solution where it bleached slowly.

2. Red No. 3 appears to be the least stable, precipitating both in an acidic solution and with calcium chloride and changing colors in all other cases.

3. Red No. 3 will precipitate at a pH of 2, so it could not be used as a colorant in a strongly acidic solution.

4. The Clorox (an oxidizing agent) caused decolorization of all the food colorants tested.

5. Synthetic food colorants appear to be stronger colorants than the natural colors tested in Activity 2. It took only one drop of the synthetic colorant to achieve a deep shade compared to four or five drops of the natural color.

6. If the yellow color was Yellow No. 6, it appears from this experiment that it would be likely to decolorize, and the students would find the socks bleached to pale yellow or white.

Activity 4: What Colorant Is Present?

This activity uses paper chromatography to separate and identify FD&C colors present in commercial products using known FD&C colors as standards.

As a companion teacher demonstration, you may wish to illustrate the effect of the changing the solvent system to provide a cleaner separation. To do so, substitute a mixture of 9 mL distilled water, 10 mL methanol (CH$_3$OH), and 1.0 g sodium chloride (NaCl) for the 0.1% NaCl solvent solution used in the student activity. Proper precautions must be taken when using methanol. (See Safety and Disposal.) Avoid student contact with the solvent or paper when it is wet.

Safety and Disposal

The candy and pistachio nuts used in the extensions must NOT be eaten. If doing the companion teacher demonstration, wear goggles and gloves and use adequate ventilation as methanol is toxic and can be absorbed through the skin. Methanol is also highly flammable and should be kept away from open flames.

Materials

Per pair of students
- 600-mL beaker
- 3 sheets chromatography paper (10-cm x 30-cm)
- pencil
- 15-cm x 15-cm square of plastic wrap
- ruler
- stapler
- set of FD&C colorants in plastic pipets (Use the same as in Activity 3.)
- 10-mL graduated cylinder
- 1.0 g sodium chloride (NaCl)
- distilled water

In most geographical locations, tap water can be substituted for distilled water in this activity. However, should you decide to use tap water, you should test the activity using tap water before performing the activity with students. Note that some colorants form insoluble calcium and magnesium salts in hard water.

Per class
- several sets of nontoxic colored markers
- packets of unsweetened Kool-Aid of various colors
- Easter-egg dyes
- commercial food colors of several different brands

Getting Ready

Prepare the 0.1% NaCl solution by dissolving 1.0 g NaCl in 1 L distilled water.

Answers to Summary Questions

1. Answers will vary according to brands used.

2. Answers will vary.

3. Answers will vary.

4. The blue colorant almost always moves with or close to the solvent front. One must conclude that the structure of the molecule is such that it is highly attracted to the solvent.

5. No. Various brands provide different chromatograms. Students should cite specific examples from their experiment.

Activity 5: Can This Be Yellow No. 6?

In this laboratory activity students will carry out the synthesis of FD&C Yellow No. 6. They will then confirm its identity using paper chromatography and compare its R_f value with that of a commercial certified sample of FD&C Yellow No. 6.

Safety and Disposal

Eye protection must be worn while preparing the solutions and during this experiment. Avoid ingestion and inhalation of the reagents used and contact with skin and eyes. If contact occurs, wash the affected area thoroughly with running water. Should contact with the eyes occur, rinse the affected area with water for 15 minutes and seek medical attention while rinsing is occurring.

Sulfanilic acid (4-aminobenzene sulfonic acid) and Schaeffer's salt (2-napthol-6-sulfonic acid, sodium salt) are used in dye chemistry. The solutions of the reagents used in this activity are made up in a sodium hydroxide solution (NaOH). Goggles, gloves, and old clothing or a lab apron should be used. Use only in a well-ventilated area.

Goggles and gloves must be worn when handling sodium nitrite ($NaNO_2$). Use only in a well-ventilated area and wash thoroughly after handling. $NaNO_2$ is an oxidizing agent. Avoid heating it or contact with combustible materials, ammonium salts, or strong reducing agents. Use under a fume hood.

Concentrated solutions of hydrochloric acid (HCl) are very corrosive. They can cause severe chemical burns. The vapor is extremely irritating to the skin, eyes, and respiratory system.

Yellow No. 6 will stain your hands and/or clothing. Wear an apron to protect clothing. Lab gloves may be worn to protect your hands.

Materials

Per pair of students
- 5 plastic transfer pipets
- 1 drop concentrated hydrochloric acid (HCl)
- finely crushed ice
- small test tube (13-mm x 100-mm)
- 1 capillary tube
- strip chromatography paper (10-cm x 12-cm)
- 600-mL beaker
- 15-cm x 15-cm square of plastic wrap
- stapler
- ruler
- apron
- (optional) lab gloves
- goggles for each student
- 10-mL graduated cylinder

Per class

- 2.9 g sulfanilic acid (4-aminobenzene sulfonic acid)
- 4.2 g 2-napthol-6-sulfonic acid, sodium salt (Schaeffer's salt)

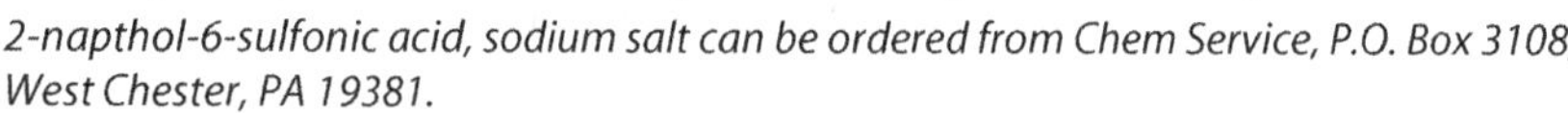

2-napthol-6-sulfonic acid, sodium salt can be ordered from Chem Service, P.O. Box 3108, West Chester, PA 19381.

- 10 g sodium hydroxide (NaOH)
- 10 g sodium nitrite ($NaNO_2$)
- several small beakers containing stock solution of FD&C Yellow No. 6

Place capillary tubes in these beakers for transferring solution to the chromatography paper.

- distilled water (Deionized water can be substituted.)
- 1.0 g sodium chloride (NaCl)

Getting Ready

1. Prepare Solution A by mixing 2.9 g sulfanilic acid (4-aminobenzene sulfonic acid), 7.5 mL 10% NaOH (dissolve 10 g NaOH in 100 mL solution), and 50 mL distilled water.

2. Prepare Solution B by mixing 9 mL 10% NaOH, 100 mL distilled water, and 4.2 g 2-napthol-6-sulfonic acid (sodium salt).

3. Prepare a 10% $NaNO_2$ solution by dissolving 10 g $NaNO_2$ in distilled water to a final volume of 100 mL.

4. Prepare a 0.1% NaCl solution by dissolving 1.0 g NaCl in distilled water to a final volume of 1L.

Answers to Summary Questions

1. Answers will vary, but colors should be very similar.

2. Chromatograms generally show experimental Yellow No. 6 to be a single component.

3. R_f values should compare favorably.

4. It would be unwise as there might be unreacted starting materials present which could be harmful. It would be illegal because any colorant to be used in food must be certified by governmental standards.

■ Supplementary Activities

Cross-Curricular Integration

Economics and History

Have students research and report on the trade implications of having different synthetic colorants approved in different countries. (For example, FD&C Red No. 40 is certified in the United States but not in the European Economic Community, EEC. In the EEC, they use Red No. 2, which is not certified in the U.S.)

Have students research and report upon the colorant certification process. How does the time and expense of the process impact upon the ultimate cost to the consumer? Does the cost of the certification process restrict the probability of further certification of colorants?

Have students research and report upon the historical controversies surrounding the certification and delisting of a synthetic color.

Have students research and report on the way in which political factors affect the availability of exempt colors (natural colors), many of which are imported from third-world countries.

Biology

Have students study color perception in animals. They could then design and carry out experiments, artificially altering the colors of dog and cat foods and testing an animal's acceptance of different-colored foods.

Interview a health professional or food scientist about human allergies to FD&C colors.

Psychology

Have students organize a more extensive research project testing color perception and preference as it relates to food choices and flavor.

Business and Marketing

Have students design marketing and ad campaigns promoting foods of unusual colors.

Have students research and report on current production and promotion of colorless carbonated beverages (e.g., New York Seltzers, Clearly Canadian, Crystal Pepsi, etc.).

References

Coultate, T.P. *Food, The Chemistry of its Components,* 2nd ed.; Royal Society of Chemistry: London, England, 1989.

Counsell, J. N., *Natural Colours for Food and Other Uses;* Applied Science Publishers: London, England, 1981.

deMan, J. M. *Principles of Food Chemistry,* 2nd ed.; Van Nostrand Rheinhold: New York, 1990.

Developments In Food Colours I; Walford, J., Ed.; Applied Science: London, England, 1980.

Harrington, G. *Real Food, Fake Food and Everything in Between;* Macmillan: New York, NY, 1987.

Markakis, P. *Anthocyanins as Food Colors;* Academic: New York, 1982.

Markow, P.G. "The Ideal Solvent for Paper Chromatography of Food Dyes," *Journal of Chemical Education.* 1988, 65, 899–90.

Marmion, D. M., *Handbook of U.S. Colorants,* 3rd ed.; John Wiley and Sons: New York, 1991.

Riddle, C., Senior Chemist, Hilton Davis, personal communication.

Thompson, S. *Chemtrek;* Allyn and Bacon: Boston, MA, 1989.

Part B: Classroom Materials

What Color Do You Taste?

Activity 1: How Does Color Affect Our Perception of Food?
Student Background 1: Uses of Food Colorants Throughout History
Overhead 1: Original and Current Approved Synthetic Colorants

Why Are Roses Red and Violets Blue?

Student Background 2: How Does Nature Color Foods?
Overhead 2: Structures of Some Natural Colors
Activity 2: How Stable Are Naturally Occurring Food Colors?

What's in the Chemist's Palette?

Student Background 3: The Chemistry of Synthetic Food Colorants
Activity 3: How Stable Are Synthetic Food Colors?
Overhead 3: Structures of Synthetic Food Colors
Activity 4: What Colorant is Present?
Activity 5: Can This Be Yellow No. 6?
Overhead 4: Synthesis of Yellow No. 6

How Do We Know It's Safe?

Student Background 4: Governmental Use Restrictions for Color Additives
Student Background 5: Risk/Benefit Analysis of Food Colorants

What Color Do You Taste?

Activity 1: How Does Color Affect Our Perception of Food?

Food and drinks, particularly vegetables and fruits, abound in color. We choose certain varieties of apples by their color: Red and Golden Delicious, Green Granny Smiths. We roast, toast, and bake dishes to give them attractive colors and garnish white potatoes with a dash of red paprika or a sprinkle of orange cheddar cheese. There are very few cookbooks printed in black and white. Color in food and drink is of universal importance.

Color is sometimes used as an indicator of the quality and condition of food. Bananas with dark brown to black skins are avoided as overripe, strawberries are not appreciated until they are a deep red. Color can also "label" flavor. In processed foods, one expects a certain color to indicate a certain flavor. (See table.)

Association Between Flavors and Colors	
Flavor	Color
apricot	pale golden yellow
butterscotch	golden brown
cherry	bright bluish red
chocolate	dark reddish brown
clove	light red
lemon	canary yellow
lime	bright bluish green
mint	light green
pineapple	light greenish yellow
pistachio	bright green
strawberry	bright pinkish red

During the commercial preparation of foods and drinks, manufacturers can control the color by the use of added coloring. Because addition of colorants costs money and adds to the complexity of the production, but also adds to the salability of the product, serious research is carried out to assess consumer preference for the coloring of foods.

One such study was conducted in 1979 in Great Britain to assess the importance of color to recognition of flavor type. Four flavored fruit drinks (orange, lemon, grapefruit and pineapple) were tasted by a panel of consumers. When all were uncolored, the panelists could correctly identify the flavors only 70% of the time, compared with 90% recognition when the colored varieties were tasted.

Color preferences for foods even carry over to the food served to pets. While it is well documented that among domestic pets, only birds can detect colors, pet food manufacturing is the second largest consumer of synthetic colorants in the United States. The consumer wants red chunks of "meat" in a rich brown "gravy" to present to Fido!

For safety reasons, the following activities, which involve the consumption of food products, must NOT be carried out in the chemistry lab. Acceptable alternatives are the school's food lab, cafeteria, or a standard classroom which has been properly cleaned.

Part 1: How Do Color Clues Help Identify Flavors?

A "test panel" will attempt to identify by flavor (not brand name) a series of colorless commercial carbonated beverages. These may include various fruit flavored seltzers and colorless colas. With no visual clues from bottles or labels, it is often difficult to distinguish between colorless carbonated beverages, since even many colas are fruit based. The test panel should record their choices without consultation and the results should be tabulated and discussed.

Part 2: Do "Wrong" Color Clues Tend to Confuse Flavors?

The test panel will attempt to identify, by flavor, gelatin cubes of mismatched flavor and color. Prepare the cubes by softening 2 packets of unflavored gelatin in 50 mL cold water and then adding 300 mL hot water and ⅓ cup sugar. Stir until the gelatin and sugar are completely dissolved. Divide the gelatin solution into several portions and add colorings and flavorings. Two to three drops of color and five to six drops of flavoring extract are enough to give a distinct color and a pronounced flavor. Examples of mismatched colors and flavor are: red gelatin flavored lemon, yellow gelatin flavored orange, green gelatin flavored pineapple. Allow the gelatin to solidify in flat pans. Cut small blocks for use in the taste test. Again the panel should record their choices and results should be tabulated and discussed.

Part 3: Is Color a Factor in the Choice of Foods?

In this activity, the test panel is presented with a choice of small cups of sherbet, clearly labeled as to flavor. Half of the samples are the traditional color associated with the flavor and the other half are white. Data is gathered as to whether the test panel more often chose the colored sample over the white, even though the white sample was clearly labeled as the same flavor.

What Color Do You Taste?

Student Background 1: Uses of Food Colorants Throughout History

Brightly colored jelly beans, red maraschino cherries, and purple bubble gum all lead us to think of food colorants as a fairly recent phenomenon. This is not the case. Egyptian tomb paintings dating to 1500 B.C. depict servants preparing colored candies and the first-century Roman historian, Pliny the Elder, noted that wines were being artificially colored as early as the fourth century B.C. In 1396, an edict published in Paris forbade the artificial coloring of butter. Interestingly, the first synthetic material approved as a food colorant in the United States in 1886 was also a colorant for butter.

In the second half of the 19th century, the use of synthetic food colorants became widespread. This trend was sparked by the discovery of synthetic dyes, beginning with William Perkin's synthesis of mauvine in 1856. By the turn of the century, 695 food colorants were in use worldwide, manufactured by 37 different firms. Most of these had no testing as to their health effects.

The "good old days" were not so good. Various colorants were introduced into food to hide poor quality or to pass off imitation foods as real. Flour, pastries, and pasta were colored yellow to conceal dirt and give the impression of high egg content, jams and jellies were colored to give the appearance of more fruit, and old meat was colored to make it look fresh. Pickles were colored with copper sulfate (blue-green); cheese rinds with lead oxide (red); and candies were shaded with red lead, lead chromate (yellow), and mercury sulfide (black). An 1880 Boston survey revealed that 46% of all candy was colored with mineral pigments, usually lead chromate. In Vienna in 1870, some 200 food samples were analyzed and 90% were found to contain arsenic, traceable to the colorant used to dye them. Many of these food additives were highly toxic. (See table.)

Toxicological Information on Early Food Colorants*	
Additive	Toxicity
copper sulfate	strong irritant to mucous membranes
red lead	acute toxicity, especially in younger children may lead to permanent brain damage
lead oxide and lead chromate	toxic in animal studies
mercury salts	acute toxicity, kidney damage, muscle tremors, depression, and nervousness
arsenic salts	acute toxicity, cumulative
*As this data gradually became available, the use of these materials was prohibited.	

It was in processed foods and manufactured confectioneries that the addition of food colorants was most widespread. As the 19th century came to a close, the United States was changing from an agricultural to an industrial economy. No longer did most Americans live on farms and produce their own food. Instead, much of the food for this nation of city dwellers was processed, chemically preserved, and marketed by large firms which competed for consumer dollars.

Dr. Harvey Wiley, named to head the USDA Bureau of Chemistry in 1883, chose as his main goal the protection of the nation's food supply and began an effort to pass legislation regulating the food industry. The Food and Drug Act of 1906 banned the addition of poisonous colorants to confectionery and prohibited the use of colorants for the purpose of concealing inferiority.

In 1906, Wiley hired the chemist Dr. Bernard C. Hesse as a consultant and gave him the mandate to determine which colorants could safely be used in food. In 1907 Hesse proposed a "short list" of seven approved colorants for use in foods and further suggested that each batch of the colorant must be certified as meeting certain standard regulations. A major revision of the Food and Drug Act signed into law in 1938 finally made batch certification mandatory and set down many of the regulations which still govern use of colorants in the food industry.

Since the early work of Bernard Hesse, various colorants have been approved for use in foods and some, as new information has become available, have been "delisted." (See table.) Currently, seven synthetic colorants are certified for use in foods, only two of which were on Hesse's original list. Colorants which are certified for use in coloring foods, drugs, and cosmetics are known as FD&C colorants.

Certified colorants are added to only about 10% of our total food supply with the major areas of usage being beverages, candy and confections, pet foods, dessert powders, and bakery goods.

Chronological History of Synthetic Food Colors in the United States			
Year Listed for Food Use	FD&C Name	Year Delisted	Currently Permitted
1907	Red No. 1	1961	no
1907	Red No. 2	1976	no
1907	Red No. 3	—	yes
1907	Orange No. 1	1956	no
1907	Yellow No. 1	1959	no
1907	Green No. 2	1966	no
1907	Blue No. 2	—	yes
1916	Yellow No. 5	—	yes
1918	Yellow No. 3	1959	no
1918	Yellow No. 4	1959	no
1922	Green No. 1	1966	no
1927	Green No. 3	—	yes
1929	Red No. 4	1976	no
1929	Yellow No. 6	—	yes
1929	Blue No. 1	—	yes
1939	Yellow No. 2	1959	no
1939	Orange No. 2	1956	no
1939	Red No. 32	1956	no
1950	Violet No. 1	1973	no
1971	Red No. 40	—	yes

What Color Do You Taste?

Overhead 1: Original and Current Approved Synthetic Colorants

Year Approved	Original Seven	Current Seven	Year Approved
1907	Red No. 1		
1907	Red No. 2		
1907	Orange No. 1		
1907	Yellow No. 1		
1907	Green No. 2		
1907	Blue No. 2	Blue No. 2	1907
1907	Red No. 3	Red No. 3	1907
		Yellow No. 5	1916
		Green No. 3	1927
		Yellow No. 6	1929
		Blue No. 1	1929
		Red No. 40	1971

Why Are Roses Red and Violets Blue?

Student Background 2: How Does Nature Color Foods?

Mother Nature herself apparently recognizes the appeal of color, for many foods are naturally colored. The bright green of spinach, the ruby red of strawberries, and the deep yellow-orange of pumpkin which add visual delight to our tables are all due to chemicals which occur naturally in those foods. Three major color groups are due to the chemical families discussed below.

The chlorophylls are the green pigments of leafy vegetables. They also give the green color to the skin of apples and other fruit, particularly when the fruit is unripe. Chlorophylls are the functional pigment of photosynthesis in all green plants. Chlorophylls a and b, shown in Figure B1, are the major members of the family found in food plants.

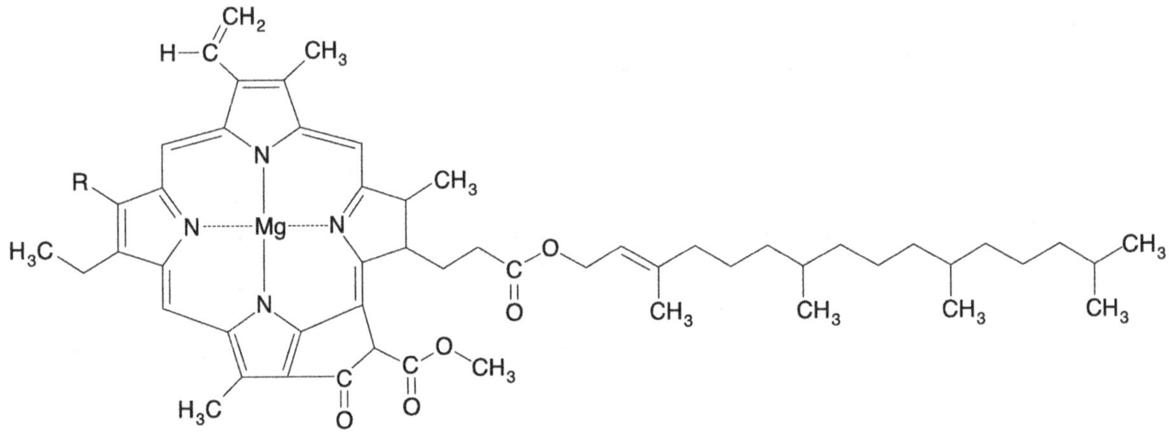

Figure B1: Chlorophylls a and b, responsible for the green color in many vegetables (chlorophyll a: R = CH₃; chlorophyll b: R = CHO)

Many conditions affect chlorophyll content, and almost any type of food processing or storage causes some change of the chlorophyll molecules and thus, some change in the color. The most common change is replacement of the central magnesium ion by hydrogen, a reaction which requires acidic conditions (Most foods are acidic) and is favored by high temperatures. The resulting compounds have a dirty brown color. Since commercial canning of vegetables such as peas involves processing at high temperatures, obtaining an acceptable color for the canned product is a significant problem.

Carotenoid pigments are responsible for most of the yellow and orange colors of fruits and vegetables. Carotenoids include two major classes: carotenes, which contain only hydrogen and carbon; and xanthophylls, which are oxygen-containing derivatives of the carotenes. (See Figure B2.) The major cause of carotenoid breakdown in food is oxidation, though carotenoids are also somewhat unstable to heat.

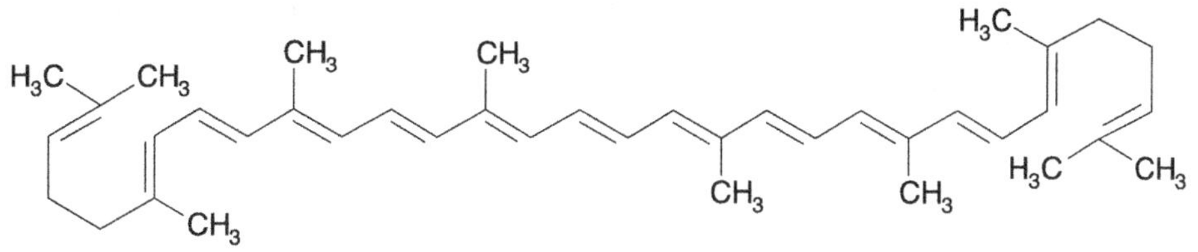

lycopene (red)

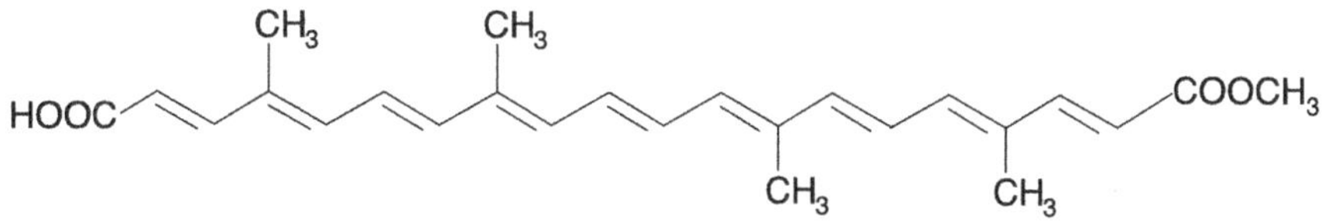

bixin (yellow)

Figure B2: Lycopene, a carotene, and bixin, a xanthophyll

Carotenoids have been thoroughly studied because beta-carotene, from which vitamin A can be derived, is an important nutrient in the human diet. Although normally associated with plants, carotenoids do find their way into some animal tissue. The yellow in egg yolk and, in smaller amounts, in animal fat, is due to carotenoids.

The pink, red, blue, and violet colors of fruits and vegetables are caused by the presence of anthocyanins. Anthocyanins are organic compounds that are usually found in the sap of epidermal plant cells. This group of compounds has very complex structures that vary widely. However, most anthocyanins found in nature contain the basic three-ring structure shown in Figure B3. This three-ring structure is called a flavylium ion.

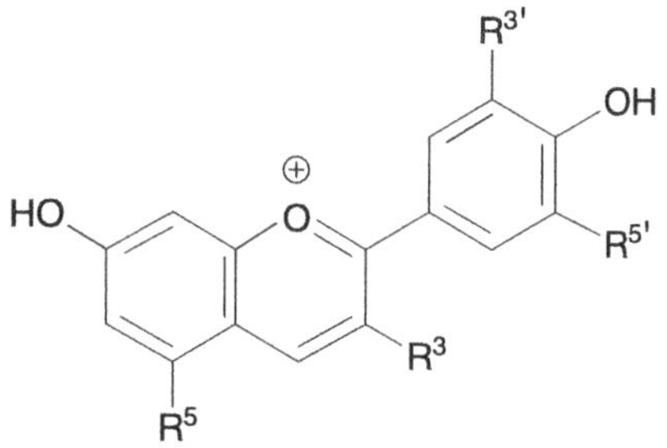

Figure B3: The general flavylium structure. The most common is cyanidin, where R^5, R^3, and $R^{5'}$=OH and $R^{3'}$=H.

Anthocyanins typically contain one or more sugar molecules attached to the flavylium ion at the R^3 and/or R^5 position. Sometimes acyl groups are attached to the sugar molecules. (See Figure B4.)

$$R-C\overset{\displaystyle O}{\diagdown}$$

Figure B4: The structure of an acyl group

Hydroxyl (–OH) and methoxy (–OCH$_3$) groups can also substitute at the R locations not otherwise containing sugar residues.

The flavylium ion is the part of the anthocyanin molecule that absorbs visible light and gives the compound its color. Various anthocyanins provide a wide range of colors, for example, if R = OH, the color tends to be more blue and if R = OCH$_3$ the color will shift towards red.

The color of anthocyanins is affected not only by the anthocyanin structure but also by pH and the concentration of the pigment. The almost black hue of eggplant skin is due to an exceedingly high concentration of an anthocyanin which in lower concentrations appears light blue. A red cabbage salad shifts from purple to bright pinkish red when an acidic vinegar dressing is added.

In most food processing operations, anthocyanins are quite stable, especially if the pH is kept fairly low. Ascorbic acid and sulfur dioxide, both widely used in food preservation, cause decolorization of anthocyanins.

Why Are Roses Red and Violets Blue?

Overhead 2: Structures of Some Natural Colors

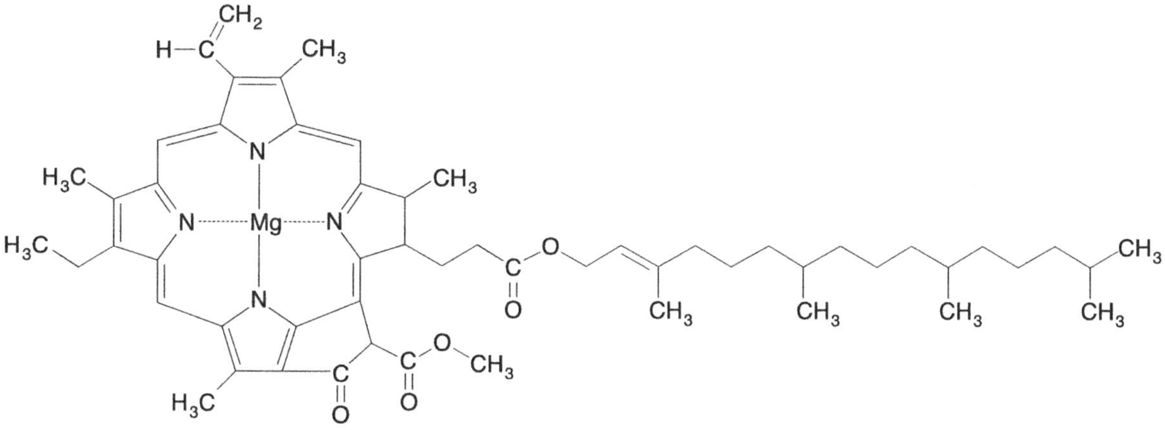

Chlorophyll a, the bluish-green colorant in many vegetables

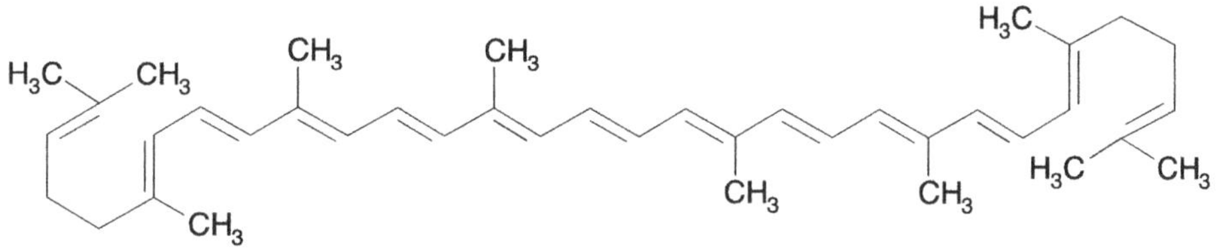

Lycopene, the red carotene color of tomatoes

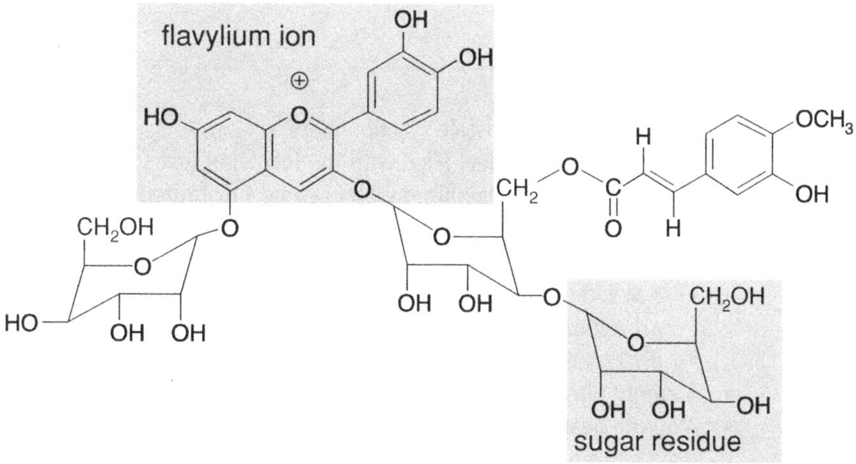

One of the anthocyanins present in red cabbage

Why Are Roses Red and Violets Blue?

Activity 2: How Stable Are Naturally Occurring Food Colors?

In the past several decades, people have become increasingly conscious of food additives in general and of food colorants in particular. The safety of synthetic food colorants has long been questioned. Certain synthetic food colors were quickly recognized as toxic with others only more recently being considered health hazards. With the move back to basics and non-processed foods, the fact that food colorants are not "natural" has also made them suspect. It is important to recognize that not all naturally colorful plants are harmless. Pokeberries, traditionally used to provide a red dye for textiles, are poisonous, as are the bright red berries of mistletoe.

Some natural materials have long been successfully used as food colorants. Annatto extract, obtained from the seeds of the Annatto tree, has been used for over 100 years as a yellow colorant for butter in both Europe and the United States. (See illustration at left.)

The possibility of using more naturally occurring colors such as the anthocyanins found in many fruits to replace synthetic food colorants is being widely studied. As with their synthetic counterparts, the possibilities for using natural colorants are limited by their chemical and physical properties. In this experiment the chemical stability of several natural colorants is investigated.

Safety

Eye protection must be worn for this experiment. Basic solutions (pH 12) are caustic and acidic solutions (pH 2) are corrosive. Contact with the skin and eyes must be avoided. Should contact occur, rinse the affected area with water for 15 minutes. If the contact involves the eyes, seek medical assistance while rinsing is occurring.

Materials

Per pair of students
- 24-well plastic microscale reaction plate
- 6 plastic transfer pipets filled with the following test solutions:
    - distilled water (Deionized water can be substituted.)
    - 1 M calcium chloride solution ($CaCl_2$)
    - 10% Clorox® solution
    - 1 M sodium thiosulfate solution ($Na_2S_2O_3$)
    - pH 2 solution
    - pH 12 solution
- 4 empty plastic transfer pipets
- 4 50-mL beakers
- glass stirring rod
- metal spatula

- small funnel and filter paper
- small piece of beet
- 1 spoonful turmeric
- 1 spoonful grape juice concentrate
- 3–4 cranberries (frozen or fresh)
- sheet of white paper
- toothpick
- 15 mL 50/50 isopropyl alcohol/water solution
- goggles for each student

Procedure

1. Prepare the natural dye solutions:

   a. Cut the piece of beet into smaller pieces with the metal spatula and place the pieces in a 50-mL beaker. Cover the pieces with 10 mL distilled water. Stir occasionally. After about 10 minutes, draw the beet juice/water mixture into a plastic transfer pipet.

   b. In a second 50-mL beaker, mix the turmeric with the 50/50 isopropyl alcohol/water solution and allow to stand for 10 minutes. Do not stir after the initial mixing so that the bulk of the solid will settle to the bottom. Decant the solution into a small funnel and filter paper and filter the solution into a clean beaker. Draw the filtered solution into a plastic transfer pipet.

   c. Dilute the grape juice concentrate with 25 mL distilled water. Draw some of the solution into a plastic transfer pipet.

   d. In a clean 50-mL beaker, crush the cranberries with a glass stirring rod. Add 10 mL distilled water and mix thoroughly. Allow to stand for 10 minutes. Draw off the transparent, colored supernatant liquid with a plastic transfer pipet.

2. Place the 24-well microscale reaction plate on a white sheet of paper. Position the plate with the long side facing you.

3. Fill each of the four wells in the six vertical columns with 15 drops of one of the test solutions: distilled water in the wells in column 1, pH 2 test solution in the wells in column 2, and so on.

4. Add 4 drops of beet extract (Step 1a) to each of the wells in the top horizontal row.

5. Add four drops of turmeric extract (Step 1b) to each well in the second horizontal row of wells.

6. Repeat the procedure with rows 3 and 4 using grape juice (Step 1c) in row 3 and cranberry juice (Step 1d) in row 4.

7. Stir each well with a toothpick, rinsing the toothpick with distilled water between wells.

8. Allow the solutions to stand for 15 minutes. Record your observations in the data table. Colors should be compared with the color in row 1, which is the control since it contains only the colorant and distilled water.

Stability of Natural Dyes in Various Liquids						
	distilled water	pH 2 solution	pH 12 solution	1 M $CaCl_2$ (aq)	10% Clorox	1 M $Na_2S_2O_3$ (aq)
beet						
turmeric						
grape						
cranberry						

Summary Questions

1. Under what conditions did the natural colors tested decolorize completely?

2. Under what conditions did the natural colors tested undergo a major color change?

3. Which of the natural colors tested appeared to be the most stable? Explain.

4. Suggest some problems which might arise when attempting to use a color extracted from beets or turmeric to color other foods.

5. A baker who was preparing cranberry bread found that the batter consistently turned a greenish color in the area around the cranberry pieces. The bread was a quick bread in which sodium bicarbonate (baking soda) was used as the leavening agent. Explain the baker's problem.

What's In the Chemist's Palette?

Student Background 3: The Chemistry of Synthetic Food Colorants

Most foods such as meat, white bread, potatoes and many fruits and vegetables are not artificially colored since their natural appearance is acceptable to consumers. Foods are typically colored either because they have no color of their own or because their natural color varies drastically with locale or season or is destroyed or changed during food processing and storage. Colorants added to such foods are intended to make them more appealing to the consumer.

The major use of color additives is to give color to otherwise colorless products. Many beverages, gelatins, candies and ice cream fall into this category. Consumers often find colorless foods unappealing and difficult to identify. Food storage may cause problems as natural pigments often deteriorate over time. The heat processing required to preserve foods often alters the natural colors of foods. For these various reasons, synthetic colorants have been added to foods for many years.

What are the criteria for a good food colorant? Of primary importance is its safety to the consumer. Manufacturers then look for compounds which are stable, will not give the food any objectionable odor or taste, are non-reactive with the food and its containers, have good coloring power, and are relatively inexpensive.

Synthetic food colorants are strictly regulated by the government on the basis of safety. At this time only seven synthetic colorants are approved, or certified, for use in food. These colorants may be grouped by the chromophore (color-giving) group which they contain.

Azo colorants are characterized by the presence of one or more azo bonds (–N=N–). FD&C Red No. 40 and FD&C Yellow No. 6 are examples of azo colorants. (See Figure B5.)

Red No. 40

Yellow No. 6

Figure B5: Azo colorants (The azo functional groups are shaded.)

Several certified colorants belong to a group known as triphenylmethanes which contain three benzene rings attached to a central carbon. FD&C Blue No. 1 is an example of a triphenylmethane. (See Figure B6.)

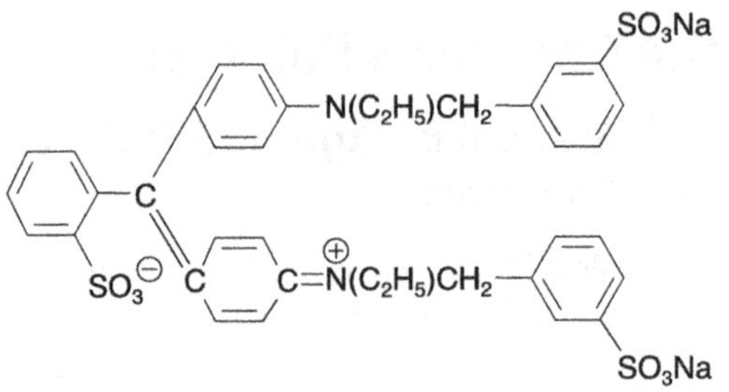

Figure B6: FD&C Blue No. 1, a triphenylmethane

FD&C Yellow No. 5, while containing an azo group, is classified as a pyrazolone because of the presence of the pyrazolone group. (See Figure B7.)

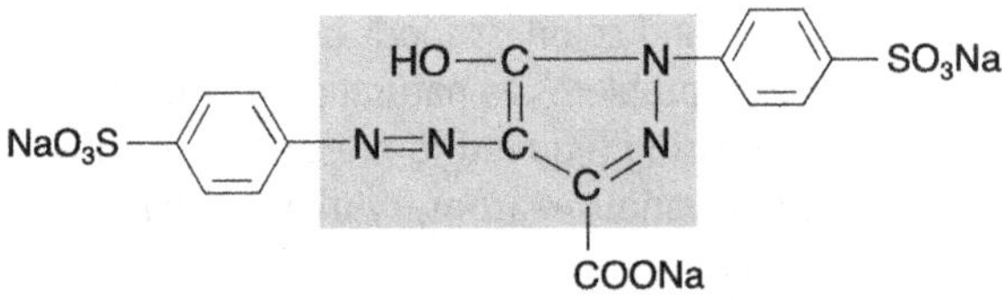

Figure B7: FD&C Yellow No. 5, a pyrazolone
(The pyrazolone group is shaded.)

Water-soluble FD&C colors are very useful in water-based foodstuffs such as beverages or gelatin desserts, but have limited use in fatty foods such as salad dressings, yogurt, and ice cream.

Lakes are a special form of color additive prepared by attaching the soluble colorant to an insoluble material, most commonly aluminum oxide. Lakes are good colorants for food products which are oil- or fat-based and are used to color such foods as candy and chewing gums, flavoring mixtures for snack foods, and various dairy products.

What's in the Chemist's Palette?

Activity 3: How Stable Are Synthetic Food Colors?

In order for a colorant to have practical use in food, it must be stable under a variety of conditions. Many colorants will decolorize in the presence of strong sunlight so it is important to protect colored foodstuffs from prolonged exposure to direct sunlight whenever possible. FD&C Red No. 3 is particularly photosensitive, its color fading within several hours. High temperatures used in food processing will also cause color loss or a change of shade, so colorants are often added as late as possible in the manufacturing process when little further heating will take place. Additionally, some colorants in the presence of "hard water" form insoluble calcium and magnesium salts.

Colorants vary widely in their stability to acids, bases, and oxidizing and reducing agents. Consider, for example, the fact that many foods which claim to contain the "minimum daily requirement" of vitamin C from ascorbic acid are colorless. Ascorbic acid, as a reducing agent, can react with many colorants, affecting their color stability. This is not to say that all colorants are decolorized by large concentrations of vitamin C. Drink powders such as Kool-Aid®, for example, are typically highly colored in spite of high vitamin C content.

In this activity, the stability of several synthetic food colorants is investigated.

Safety

Eye protection must be worn for this experiment. Basic solutions (pH 12) are caustic and acidic solutions (pH 2) are corrosive. Contact with the skin and eyes must be avoided. Should contact occur, rinse the affected area with water for 15 minutes. If the contact involves the eyes, seek medical assistance while rinsing is occurring.

Materials

Per pair of students
- 24-well plastic microscale reaction plate
- white sheet of paper
- toothpick
- 10 plastic transfer pipets, each containing one of the following:
  - distilled water (Deionized water can be substituted.)
  - 1 M calcium chloride solution ($CaCl_2$)
  - 10% Clorox solution
  - 1 M sodium thiosulfate solution ($Na_2S_2O_3$)
  - pH 2 solution
  - pH 12 solution
  - FD&C Yellow No. 6
  - FD&C Red No. 3
  - FD&C Blue No. 1
  - FD&C Red No. 40
- goggles for each student

Procedure

1. Place the microplate on a white sheet of paper. Position the plate with the long side facing you.

2. Fill each of the four wells in each of the six columns (vertical) with 15 drops of one of the six test liquids: distilled water in column 1, pH 2 solution in column 2, pH 12 solution in column 3, and so on.

3. To the top row (horizontal) of wells, add one drop of FD&C Yellow No. 6 solution to each well.

4. To the second row of wells, add one drop of FD&C Red No. 3 solution to each well.

5. Repeat the procedure in rows three and four, with FD&C Blue No. 1 in row 3 and FD&C Red No. 40 in row 4.

6. Stir each well with a toothpick, rinsing the toothpick with distilled water between wells.

7. Allow the solutions to stand for 15 minutes and record your observations in the data table. Colors should be compared with the color in column 1 which is the control since it contains only the colorant and distilled water.

Stability of Synthetic Food Colors in Several Liquids						
	distilled water	pH 2 solution	pH 12 solution	1 M $CaCl_2$ (aq)	10% Clorox	1 M $Na_2S_2O_3$ (aq)
FD&C Yellow No. 6						
FD&C Red No. 3						
FD&C Blue No. 1						
FD&C Red No. 40						

Summary Questions

1. Which of the four food colors tested appeared to be most chemically stable? Explain.

2. Which of the four food colors tested appeared to be the least chemically stable? Explain.

3. What food color cannot be used at a pH of 2? Why?

4. Which reagent appears to cause major decolorization problems for the food colors tested? Explain.

5. Compare the relative strength of the synthetic colorants in this experiment with that of the natural colorants in Activity 2.

6. By accident, a student placed a yellow pair of socks in a wash load of white clothes. When the clothes were washed, bleach was added to the load to remove stains from the white clothes. What would you predict would happen to the yellow socks?

What's in the Chemist's Palette?

Overhead 3: Structures of Synthetic Food Colors

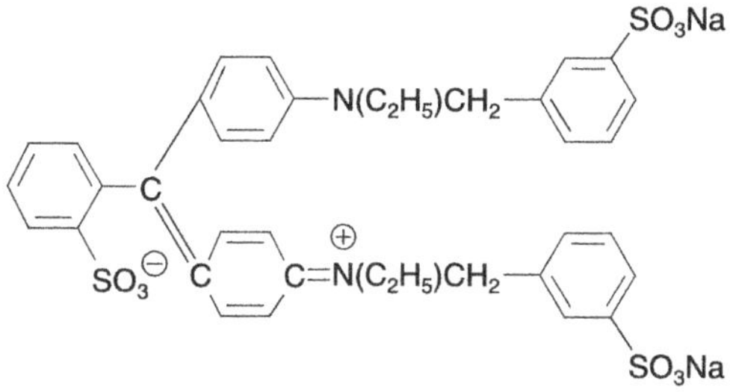

FD&C Blue No. 1

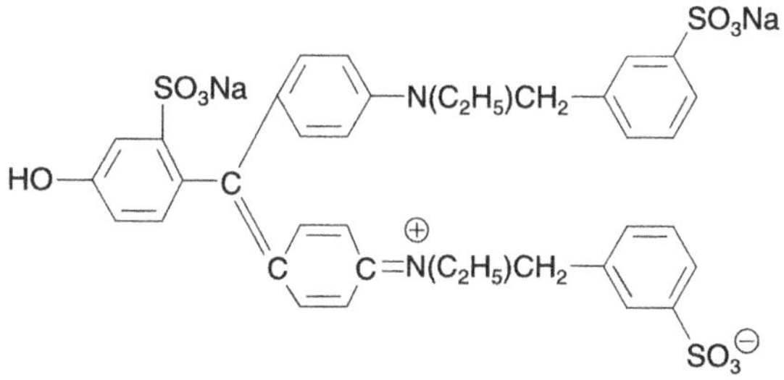

FD&C Green No. 3

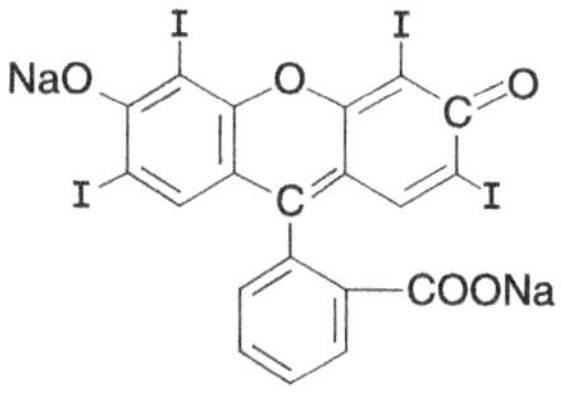

FD&C Red No. 3

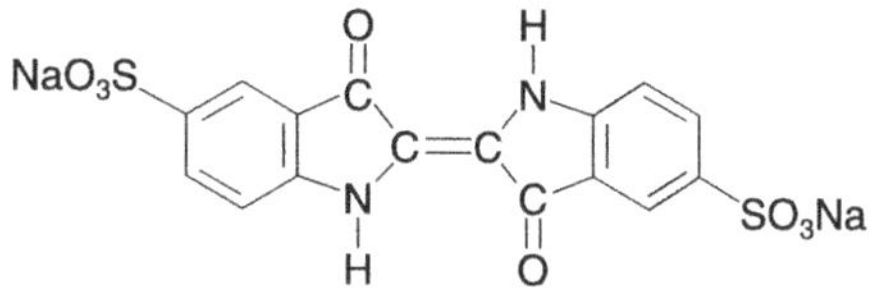

FD&C Blue No. 2

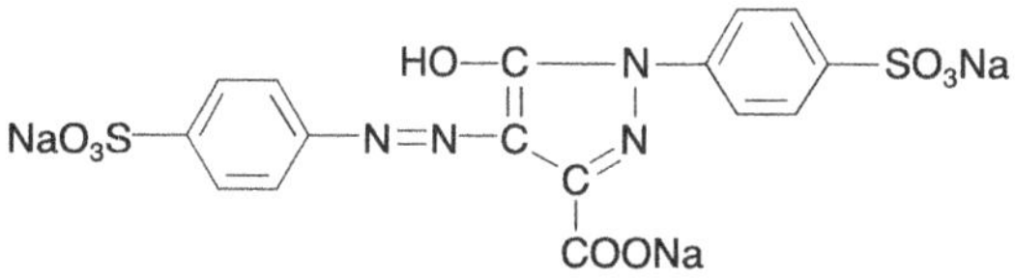

FD&C Yellow No. 5

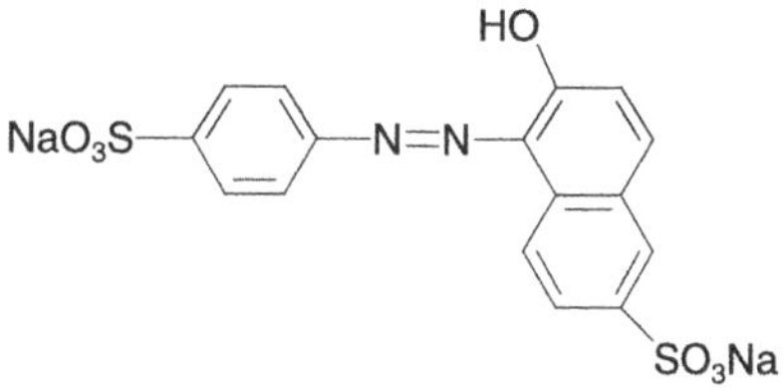

FD&C Yellow No. 6

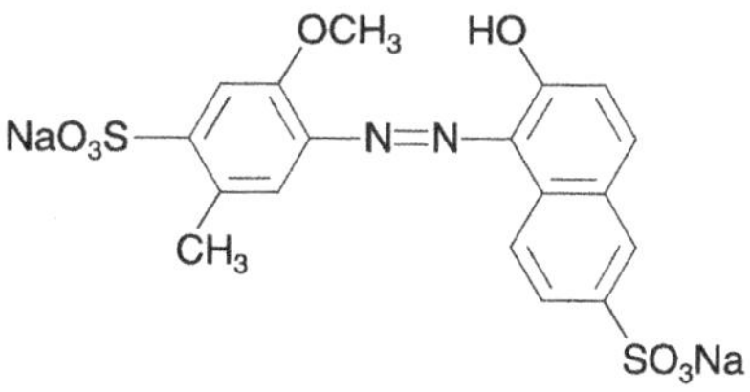

FD&C Red No. 40

What's in the Chemist's Palette?

Activity 4: What Colorant Is Present?

Chromatography is a method used for separating substances in a mixture. The name comes from the fact that this method was first used to separate colored mixtures: the Greek word *chromos* means color. Today the method is applied to many different kinds of mixtures, but the separations are easily seen if the components of the mixture are colored.

Chromatographic separation makes use of a stationary phase and a mobile phase. Separation of the mixture occurs when one component is more attracted to the mobile phase and moves along with it, while another component is more highly attracted to the stationary phase so its progress through the system is retarded.

In this experiment paper chromatography is used to separate and identify various food colorants. Chromatography paper is used as the stationary phase and a water/sodium chloride solution is used as the mobile phase. Food colorants which are water soluble are more or less tightly adsorbed onto the surface fibers of the paper. A spot of color is placed near the bottom of the chromatography paper and the end of the paper placed into a thin layer of the solvent. As the solvent moves along the paper by capillary action, each colorant (solute) travels at its own speed depending on its attraction to both the mobile phase—the solvent, and the stationary phase—the paper. Differences in these attractive forces among various colorants cause some to move faster than others, separating one from another as they move up the paper.

The distance that a substance moves relative to the movement of the solvent is called the R_f value (retention factor). The retention factor of any solute depends upon the particular solvent and paper combination. Porosity and thickness of the paper and the type of solvent used will determine the numerical R_f value of a solute. Using a set of known food colorants as reference and a standard paper/solvent combination, one can use the R_f value of colorants as an identification tool.

Safety

No special safety procedures are required.

Materials

Per pair of students
- 600-mL beaker
- 3 sheets chromatography paper (10-cm x 30-cm)
- pencil
- 15-cm x 15-cm square of plastic wrap
- ruler
- stapler

- set of FD&C food colorants in plastic pipets
- 10-mL graduated cylinder
- 20 mL of 0.1% sodium chloride (NaCl) solution

Per class
- several sets of nontoxic colored markers
- packets of unsweetened Kool-Aid® of various colors
- Easter-egg dyes
- commercial food colors of several different brands

Procedure

Colored markers that are labeled "nontoxic" must use FD&C colorants. A standard set of food colorants will be used to identify the components in some nontoxic markers.

1. With the long side of a sheet of chromatography paper facing you, use a ruler and PENCIL to draw a line the length of the paper approximately 1 cm from the bottom edge. Do NOT use pen as the ink may dissolve in the solvent and interfere with the experiment.

2. Beginning 3 cm from one end of the line, place one drop of each of the standard food colorants 2 cm apart on the line. Label each spot in pencil.

3. Continue along the line, placing a dot of color from each of the markers at each 2-cm mark. Label each color in pencil. (See Figure B8.)

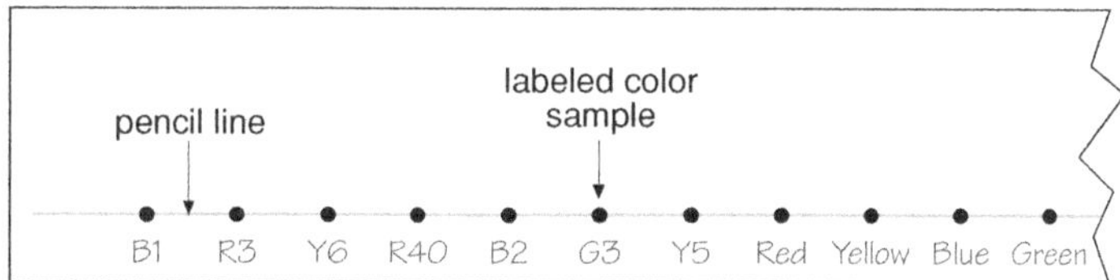

Figure B8: Marked chromotagraphy paper

4. Form a cylinder of the chromatography paper with the ends of the paper just meeting. Do not overlap. Staple the ends together at top and bottom. (See Figure B9.)

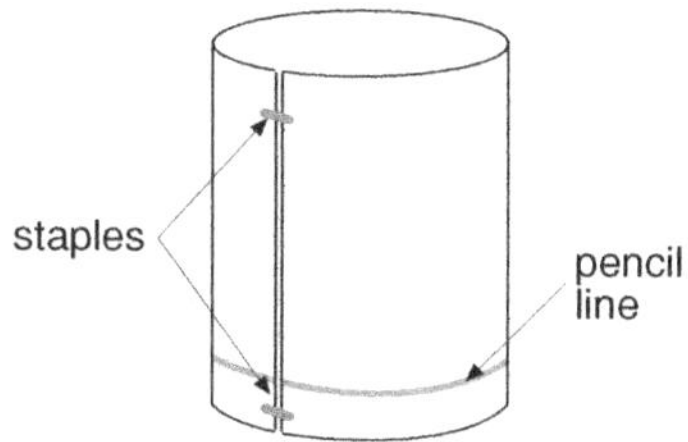

Figure B9: Chromatography cylinder

5. Pour 20 mL of 0.1% NaCl solution into the 600 mL beaker and carefully place the cylinder in the beaker. Note that the line with the colored dots MUST be above the liquid level or the colors will just dissolve in the solvent instead of traveling up the paper. Cover the top of the beaker tightly with the plastic wrap. (See Figure B10.)

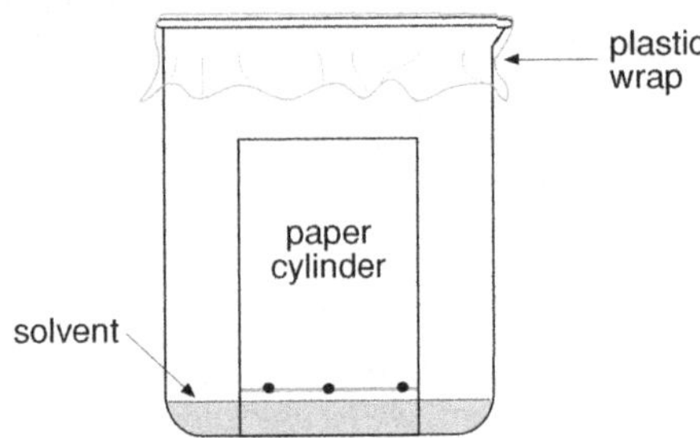

Figure B10: Beaker with chromatography paper

6. Observe that as the solution moves up the paper, the colorants move also, some more rapidly than others.

7. When the advancing front of the solvent is about 1 cm from the top of the paper (this will take about 15 minutes), uncover the beaker and carefully remove the paper cylinder.

8. Remove the staples and lay the paper on a clean surface.

9. Use a pencil to mark the location of the solvent front and the top and bottom of each band of color.

10. Measure the distance from the line of origin to the edge of the solvent front. This is the distance the solvent traveled.

11. Measure the distance from the line of origin to approximately the middle of each band of color for each of the standard food color components. For each marker, outline the various color bands that appear and measure the distance from the origin line to the approximate center of each band of color. These measurements give the approximate value for the distance each color or color component traveled. (See Figure B11.)

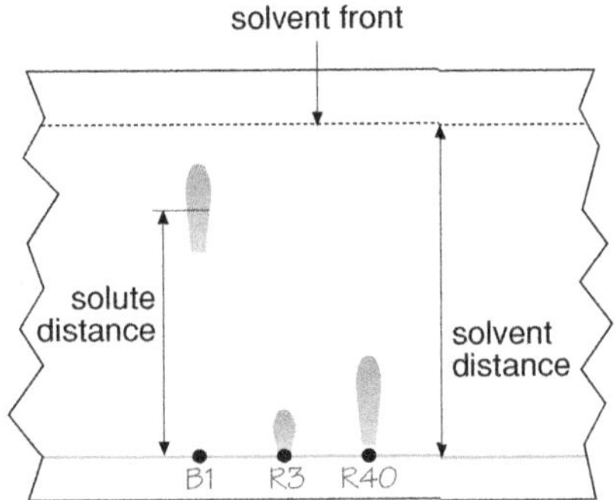

Figure B11: Completed chromatograms

12. Calculate the R_f value for each color or color component using the following formula:

$$R_f = \frac{\textit{distance solute moved}}{\textit{distance solvent moved}}$$

13. Repeat the experiment using two or three brands of commercial food colors instead of the markers to determine if the formulation for commercial food colorants is identical.

14. Repeat the experiment using unsweetened Kool-Aid® (1 heaping spoonful in 5 mL water) or Easter-egg dyes to determine which FD&C dyes are present.

Chromatography of FD&C Colors and Marker Colors			
Colorant	Solute Distance	Solvent Distance	R_f
FD&C			
Markers			

Summary Questions

1. Which colored markers appear to be composed of a single colorant and which appear to be composed of several colored components? Explain your reasoning.

2. Which marker color(s) contain FD&C Yellow No. 6?

3. Which marker color(s) contain FD&C Blue No. 1?

4. Which colorant appears to be most attracted to the water? Why? What do you conclude about the structure of the molecule that makes up that colorant?

5. Are all commercial food colors prepared with the same formulation of FD&C colorants? Explain.

Extensions

1. Pistachio nuts are often artificially colored bright red. Soak the shells of some red pistachio nuts in a small amount of water and, using paper chromatography, attempt to identify the red colorant which extracts into the water.

2. Extract the color from the surface of M&M®'s and develop chromatograms of these colors. Place an M&M in 5–6 drops of water in a 3-ounce plastic cup. Stir and turn the candy until the white layer becomes visible. Rinse the color off three more pieces of same-colored M&M's in the same water. This liquid is the color extract. Repeat this procedure with three different colors of M&M's. Using a 0.1% NaCl solution as a solvent, develop chromatograms of each color extract on filter paper.

■ What's in the Chemist's Palette?

Activity 5: Can This Be Yellow No. 6?

FD&C Yellow No. 6 is a synthetic food colorant belonging to the azo group. The chromophore which gives it color is the –N=N– group. Yellow No. 6 is synthesized by a coupling reaction between 4-aminobenzene sulfonic acid and 2-napthol-6-sulfonic acid. The general reaction is given in Figure B12.

Figure B12: Synthesis of FD&C Yellow No. 6

Safety

Eye protection must be worn during this experiment. Avoid ingestion and inhalation of the reagents used and contact with skin and eyes. If contact occurs, wash the affected area thoroughly with running water. Should contact with the eyes occur, rinse the affected area with water for 15 minutes and seek medical attention while rinsing is occurring.

Sulfanilic acid (4-aminobenzene sulfonic acid) and Schaeffer's salt (2-napthol-6-sulfonic acid, sodium salt) are used in dye chemistry. The solutions of the reagents used in this activity are made up in a sodium hydroxide solution (NaOH). Goggles, gloves, and old clothing or a lab apron should be used. Use only in a well-ventilated area.

Goggles and gloves must be worn when handling sodium nitrite ($NaNO_2$). Use only in a well-ventilated area and wash thoroughly after handling. $NaNO_2$ is an oxidizing agent. Avoid heating it or contact with combustible materials ammonium salts, or strong reducing agents. Use under a fume hood.

Concentrated solutions of hydrochloric acid (HCl) are very corrosive. They can cause severe chemical burns. The vapor is extremely irritating to the skin, eyes, and respiratory system.

Yellow No. 6 will stain your hands and/or clothing. Wear an apron to protect clothing. Lab gloves may be worn to protect your hands.

Materials

Per pair of students
- 5 plastic transfer pipets, each containing one of the following:
  - Solution A: sulfanilic acid (4-aminobenzene sulfonic acid) dissolved in sodium hydroxide (NaOH)
  - Solution B: Schaeffer's salt (2-napthol-6-sulfonic acid) dissolved in NaOH
  - 10% $NaNO_2$ solution
  - concentrated hydrochloric acid (HCl)
  - distilled water (Deionized water can be substituted.)
- finely crushed ice
- small test tube (13 mm x 100 mm)
- 1 capillary tube
- strip of chromatography paper (10 cm x 15 cm)
- 600-mL beaker
- 15-cm x 15-cm square of plastic wrap
- 20 mL 0.1% sodium chloride solution (NaCl)
- stapler
- ruler
- apron
- (optional) lab gloves
- goggles for each student

Per class
- several small beakers containing stock solution of FD&C Yellow No. 6 with capillary tubes for spotting the chromatography paper

Procedure

1. Place 5 drops of solution A into a small test tube. Add enough finely crushed ice to double the volume in the test tube.

2. Add 2 drops 10% $NaNO_2$ and 1 drop concentrated HCl to solution A. Shake gently to mix.

3. Add 10 drops of solution B and 10 drops distilled water and mix. The formation of a deep red-orange color is evidence of Yellow No. 6.

4. Prepare the chromatography sheet by drawing a pencil line 1 cm from one edge of the long side.

5. Draw a small amount of the Yellow No. 6 prepared in Step 3 into a capillary tube. Place one drop of it on the line you have just drawn on the chromatography paper by touching the tip of the capillary tube to the line. Label the spot with pencil.

6. From the beaker of FD&C Yellow No. 6 provided as a standard, and using the capillary tube provided with that beaker, place a spot of the standard FD&C Yellow No. 6 on the line, approximately 2 cm away from the spot from Step 5. Label the spot in pencil. (See Figure B13.)

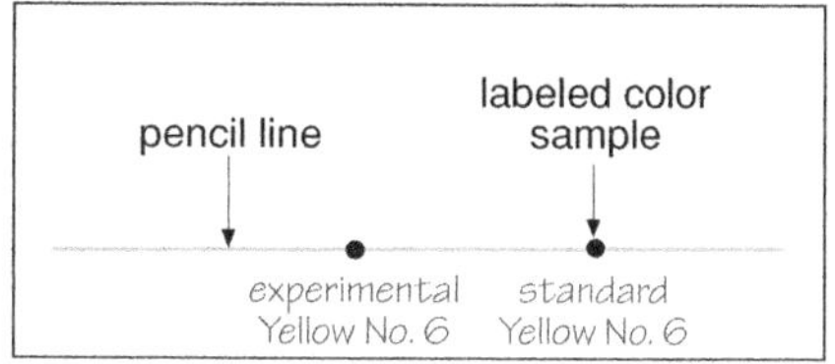

Figure B13: Paper chromatography sheet

7. Form a cylinder of the chromatography paper with the ends just meeting and staple the top and bottom. (See Figure B14.)

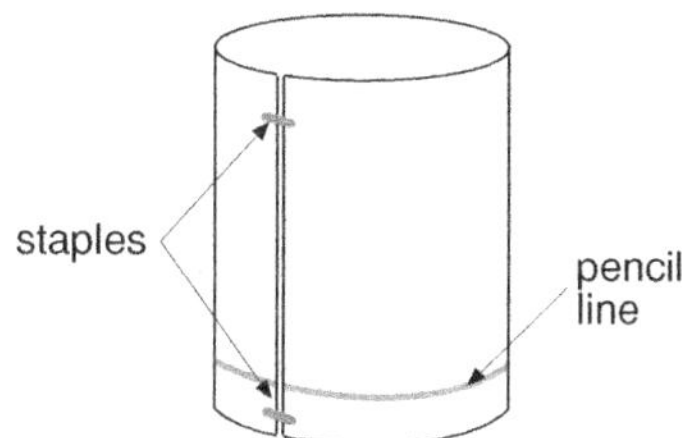

Figure B14: Chromatography cylinder

8. Pour the 1% NaCl solution into the 600-mL beaker and carefully place the cylinder in the beaker. Note that the line with the dots MUST be above the liquid level or the colors will just dissolve in the solvent instead of traveling up the paper. Cover the top of the beaker tightly with the plastic wrap. (See Figure B15.)

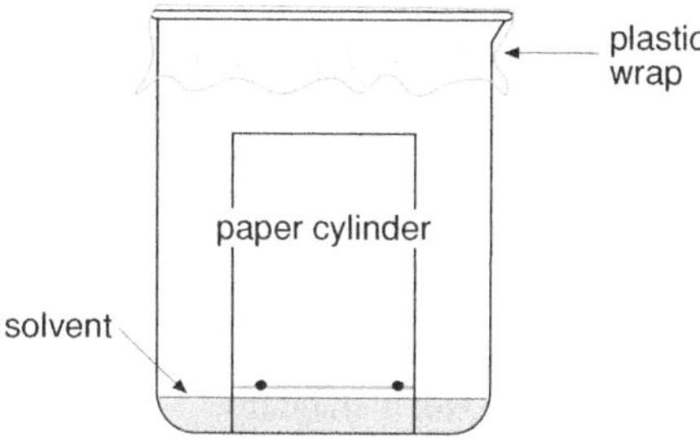

Figure B15: Beaker with chromatography paper

9. Observe the solvent as it moves up the paper by capillary action. When the advancing front of the solvent is about 1 cm from the top of the paper (This will take about 15 minutes), uncover the beaker and carefully remove the cylinder.

10. Remove the staples and lay the paper on a clean surface.

11. Use a pencil to mark the location of the solvent front.

12. Measure the distance from the line of origin to the edge of the solvent front. This is the distance the solvent traveled.

13. Measure the distance from the line or origin to approximately the middle of the color band for each of the samples. This gives an approximate value for the distance each sample (solute) traveled. (See Figure B16.)

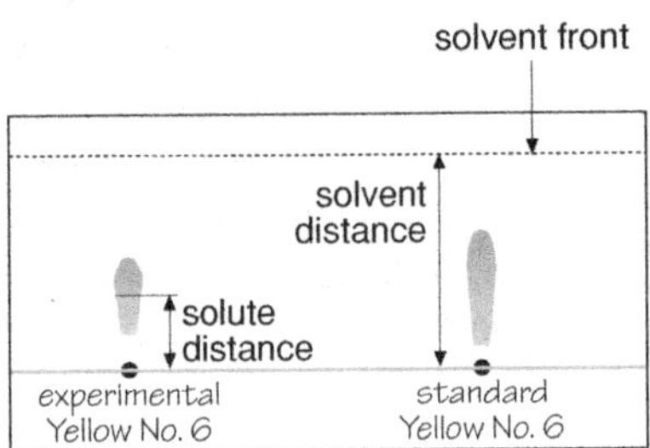

Figure B16: Measurements of solute and solvent distance

14. Calculate the R_f value for the FD&C Yellow No. 6 standard and for the Yellow No. 6 prepared experimentally.

Chromatography of FD&C Yellow No. 6 and Experimental Yellow No. 6			
Colorant	Solute Distance	Solvent Distance	R_f
FD&C Yellow No. 6			
Experimental No. 6			

Summary Questions

1. How did the Yellow No. 6 prepared experimentally compare in color with the standard FD&C Yellow No. 6 solution?

2. On examination of the chromatogram, does the experimental Yellow No. 6 appear to be a pure color? Explain.

3. Compare the R_f value of the experimental Yellow No. 6 with that for the FD&C Yellow No. 6 standard.

4. Why would it be a) unwise and b) illegal to use the Yellow No. 6 prepared in this experiment as a colorant for food?

What's in the Chemist's Palette?

Overhead 4: Synthesis of Yellow No. 6

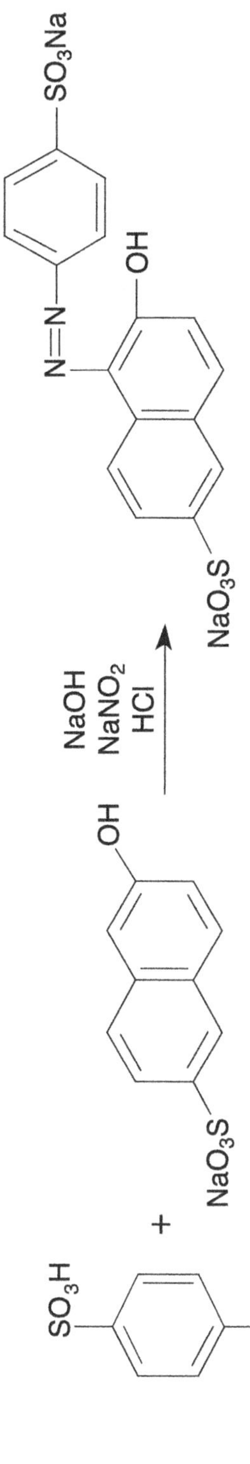

4-aminobenzene sulfonic acid

2-napthol-6-sulfonic acid

Yellow No. 6

◼ How Do We Know It's Safe?

Student Background 4: Governmental Use Restrictions for Color Additives

The rules governing color additives are complex and constantly changing. Currently, from a legal standpoint, colorants are divided into the following categories:

- FD&C Colors and Lakes: certified for use in coloring foods, drugs, and cosmetics;
- D&C Colors: colors and pigments considered safe for use in drugs and cosmetics when ingested or in contact with the mucous membranes;
- Ext. D&C Colors: for external use only; and
- Exempt Colors: need not be certified.

In general, only synthetic organic colorants are now subject to certification. Natural organic or inorganic colorants such as turmeric, fruit juices, and titanium dioxide (the white undercoating on M&M candies) are exempt from certification.

If a colorant requires certification, a sample of each batch produced must be sent to the Food and Drug Administration Color Certification Labs in Washington, DC, to determine that it conforms to prescribed specifications.

In addition to certification, numerous restrictions are placed on the use of color additives. For example, it is illegal to use them to deceive the public by adding weight or bulk to a product or by hiding quality.

The amount of color additive allowed in a product depends on both the colorant and the product. For example, titanium dioxide, TiO_2, when used to color foods cannot exceed 1% by weight of the food product. Other restrictions pertain only to specific cases. Citrus Red No. 2, for example, can only be used to color the skins of oranges not intended for processing.

Regulations regarding safety testing *methods* vary from country to country. A colorant which is accepted as safe in one country may not be allowed by another country. FD&C Red No. 40 is used in the United States instead of Red No. 2, which was removed from the certified list in 1976. Most of the rest of the world, however, recognizes Red No. 2 as acceptable but considers Red No. 40 suspect.

How Do We Know It's Safe?

Student Background 5: Risk/Benefit Analysis of Food Colorants

When one discusses any additive for food, the question of "how safe is safe" will inevitably arise. Balancing the risk against the benefit of an action is something we do every day. We decide whether or not to drive when it is icy or whether or not to study for a possible pop quiz in tomorrow's chemistry class. Answers depend on the situation.

The problem of choosing what is reasonably safe for food additives is not an easy one. Because health risks are very emotional and very important issues, the tendency of regulatory agencies is to err on the side of caution. Unfortunately, there are no tests which will prove "absolute safety." In 1960 a much-debated Food Additives Amendment was added to the Federal Food, Drug and Cosmetics Act. A special amendment, known as the Delaney clause, specifically directed that no colorant could be approved if it could be shown to induce cancer in humans or animals *at any concentration*. This is exceedingly restrictive as it means an additive may be delisted even if the concentrations in question are many times the levels which would normally be consumed.

Producers and consumers of color additives are required, by law, to provide extensive scientific data concerning testing methods used to determine the safety of a color additive. Because of the expense involved, many colors which had been previously certified were eventually delisted because firm data was not available concerning their "absolute safety."

There must always be control over the food we eat and the additives used in food. When human health is at stake, chemicals and processes should be carefully regulated. However, regulations should include examination of competent scientific evidence. There must be realistic standards that make room for benefits as well as risks. Choices must be made as free from emotionalism as possible and with careful consideration of all the evidence.

Addressing the National Standards

Activity 1: How Does Color Affect Our Perception of Food?

Activity: Students examine the role color plays in identifying and choosing foods.

Science as Inquiry Standards

Abilities Necessary to Do Science
- Students conduct a scientific investigation into the role that color plays in choosing food.
- Communicate and defend a scientific argument. Students collect data in several trials and discuss their results as a class.

Activity 2: How Stable Are Naturally Occurring Food Colors?

Activity: The possibility of using more naturally occurring colors to replace synthetic food colorants is being widely studied. As with their synthetic counterparts, the possibilities for using natural colorants are limited by their chemical and physical properties. In this experiment the chemical stability of several natural colorants is investigated.

Science as Inquiry Standards

Abilities Necessary to Do Scientific Inquiry
- Students conduct an investigation to determine the stability of several natural colorants under various conditions.

Physical Science Standards

Chemical Reactions
- Chemical reactions occur all around us. Students investigate several possible chemical reactions that natural colorants can undergo.
- A large number of important reactions involve the transfer of either electrons (oxidation/reduction reactions) or hydrogen ions (acid/base reactions) between reacting ions, molecules, or atoms. In this activity students test natural colorants under several different conditions, including acidic, basic, oxidizing, and reducing.

Science and Technology Standards

Understandings about Science and Technology
- Creativity, imagination, and a good knowledge base are all required in the work of science. In this activity students are asked to use prior knowledge to explain why the most stable natural colorant would most likely not be used to color other foods.

Activity 3: How Stable Are Synthetic Food Colors?

Activity: In order for a colorant to have practical use in food, it must be stable under a variety of conditions. Colorants vary widely in their stability to acids, bases, and oxidizing and reducing agents. In this activity, students investigate the stability of several synthetic food colorants.

Abilities Necessary to Do Scientific Inquiry
* Students conduct an investigation to determine the stability of several synthetic colorants under various conditions.
* Students are asked to formulate scientific predictions for what would happen to a synthetic colorant under certain conditions. They are asked to explain their predictions based on evidence gained from this activity.

Physical Science Standards

Chemical Reactions
* Chemical reactions occur all around us. Students investigate several possible chemical reactions that synthetic colorants can undergo.
* A large number of important reactions involve the transfer of either electrons (oxidation/reduction reactions) or hydrogen ions (acid/base reactions) between reacting ions, molecules, or atoms. In this activity students test synthetic colorants under several different conditions, including acidic, basic, oxidizing, and reducing.

Activity 4: What Colorant Is Present?

Activity: This activity uses paper chromatography to separate and identify FD&C colors present in commercial products using known FD&C colors as standards.

Science as Inquiry Standards

Abilities Necessary to Do Scientific Inquiries
* Students conduct an investigation using paper chromatography to determine the FD&C colors present in commercial products.
* Students use mathematics to calculate the retention factor (R_f) of the colors separated by the chromatography. The R_f of the FD&C standards is compared to the colors separated from commercial products to determine the presence of FD&C colors in these products.
* Students formulate and revise scientific explanations and models using logic and evidence from their investigation. Students compare chromatographs to determine which colors were used to make different commercial products and which are most attracted to water.

Understandings about Scientific Inquiry
* Scientists inquire about how designed systems function. Students use paper chromatography to determine how colors found in commercial products are formulated.

Physical Science Standards

Structure and Properties of Matter
* The physical properties of compounds reflect the nature of the interactions among molecules. Due to intermolecular forces between molecules of various pigments, pigments can often be separated from mixtures.

Motions and Forces
* The electric force is a universal force that exists between any two charged

particles; opposite charges attract and the strength of the force is proportional to the charges. Each pigment from a mixture travels up paper at its own speed depending on its attraction for the mobile phase (solvent) and the stationary phase (paper).

Activity 5: Can This Be Yellow No. 6?

Activity: In this activity students carry out the synthesis of FD&C Yellow No. 6. They then confirm its identity using paper chromatography and compare its R_f value with that of a commercially certified sample of FD&C Yellow No. 6.

Science as Inquiry Standards

Abilities Necessary to Do Scientific Inquiry
- Students conduct an investigation to confirm the identity of the FD&C Yellow No. 6 made in the first part of this activity.
- Students use mathematics to calculate the retention factor (R_f) of both the experimental and standard FD&C Yellow No. 6.
- Students formulate and revise scientific explanations and models using logic and evidence from their investigation. Students compared chromatographs to determine if the compound made in the first part of this activity is FD&C Yellow No. 6.

Physical Science Standards

Structure and Properties of Matter
- The physical properties of compounds reflect the nature of the interactions among molecules. Due to intermolecular forces between molecules of various pigments, pigments can often be separated from a mixture through chromatography.

Motions and Forces
- The electric force is a universal force that exists between any two charged particles; opposite charges attract and the strength of the force is proportional to the charges. Each pigment in the sample travels up paper at its own speed depending on its attraction for the mobile phase (solvent) and the stationary phase (paper).

Science in Personal and Social Perspectives Standards

Natural and Human Induced Hazards
- Natural and human-induced hazards present the need for humans to assess potential danger and risk. In this activity students are asked to consider and explain why the experimental FD&C Yellow No. 6 prepared should not be used as a food colorant.

Made in the USA
Monee, IL
07 July 2026